COSTUMING THE CHRISTMAS & EASTER PLAY

With Ideas for Other Biblical Dramas

Alice M. Staeheli

Illustrations by
ROBERT WALTON & SHARON STATEMA

Christmas Photographs by
ROBERT HENDRICKS

All Other Photographs by
NORMAN CWIEK

mp

MERIWETHER PUBLISHING LTD
Colorado Springs, Colorado

Meriwether Publishing Ltd., Publisher
Box 7710
Colorado Springs, CO 80933

Editor: Arthur Zapel
Typesetting: Sharon Garlock
Cover design: Michelle Zapel Gallardo

© Copyright MCMLXXXVIII Meriwether Publishing Ltd.
Printed in the United States of America
Third Edition

Library of Congress Cataloging-in-Publication Data

Staeheli, Alice M.
    Costuming the Christmas & Easter play : with ideas
for other Biblical dramas.

    Bibliography: p.
    Includes index.
    1. Costume.   2. Christmas plays—Presentation, etc.
3. Christian drama—Presentation, etc.   4. Drama in
Christian education.   I. Walton, Robert.   II. Statema,
Sharon.   III. Title.   IV. Title: Costuming the
Christmas and Easter play.
PN2067.S73   1988   792'.026   86-43239
ISBN 0-916260-09-7

7 8 9   99 98

for Glenn:

like Bartholomew,
a steadfast encourager
like Hur,
a faithful upholder
like Jacob,
a loving husband

ACKNOWLEDGEMENT

Grateful acknowledgement for permission to use copyrighted material is made to the following:

Church Teachers Magazine, for the ideas and excerpts from the article, "Costuming the Christmas Play — Worthily" which appeared Nov. 1978, (Vol. 6, No. 3), Copyright Association of Church Teachers.

Charles Scribner's Sons, for the costume drawing of the Egyptian lady, Figure 5, and for the Roman lady, Figure 35, from *The Mode in Costume* by R. Turner Wilcox, Copyright 1942, 1948, R. Turner Wilcox; copyrights renewed 1970, 1976.

E. P. Dutton, Inc. for the costume drawing of the Assyrian costume, Figures 16 and 17, from *Dressing the Part* by Fairfax Proudfit Walkup, Copyright 1938, published by Appleton-Century-Crofts.

Meriwether Publishing Ltd. and Louise Ulmer for costume ideas from Chapter Four of her book, *Theatrecraft for Church and School,* Copyright 1982.

TABLE OF CONTENTS

CHAPTER 1:

WHAT THIS BOOK
IS ALL ABOUT

"We'll just borrow a lot of bathrobes, put the striped ones on Joseph and the shepherds and the plain ones on the Wise Men. We'll put a hole in the middle of a sheet for the heads of Mary and the angels."

"Won't they look like ghosts?"

"Not if we tie tinsel around the waist and head. That's the best we can do."

And so the curtain rises on another church Christmas pageant.

But is that the best that can be done?

The answer is a resounding "NO!" That is not the best that can, or even should be done. While the charm of the performers, the tolerance of the audience and their familiarity with the age-old story may carry the production, such slip-shod costuming does not honor the magnificent drama which is unfolded throughout the pages of the Bible. It may, in fact, detract from the beauty and meaning of the message, and at the very least, stand as living proof of a common belief that anything we can get by with is good enough for the Sunday School.

There is much to be said about the currently popular "Readers Theatre," where the audience is expected to imagine the staging and costuming. Jesus Christ can become a powerful figure for today's world when dressed in contemporary clothing, mingling with people you know. And certainly the ease and fun of the production stimulates church members to use this art form more readily.

However, there is still a place for traditional staging and production. Who can deny the uplifting magic and beauty of a well produced and costumed drama? The audience can easily be trans-

1

ported back through the centuries, carried along with the action and inspired by the message. This is especially true in respect to the Christmas and Easter stories. How else can one explain the impact and endurance of the Passion Plays that have been presented for generations?

There is an additional reason for the costumed play, especially true for amateurs. Proper costuming aids immeasurably in portraying a character. It is easier for a Wise Man to be regal, vested in stately and luxurious regalia, than when dressed in jeans and sweat shirt. And an angel is certainly more ethereal in a flowing gown than in slacks and a turtle-neck sweater.

No doubt the difficulty and outright dilemma of enticing someone to make the garments and then discovering how to make them has led either to giving up on the whole project or settling for sloppy and sometimes ridiculous costuming.

Effective costuming takes work — a great deal of work, to be candid. And it takes determination to do it well and not give in to the temptation of ignoring the details that put the "frosting on the cake." Sometimes people fail to accomplish their assigned task, and failures at the last moment bring surrender.

But cheer up! There is help at hand! No need to bite your nails and ruin your hair-do. And there is no need to bankrupt the church budget to come up with appropriate costumes. This book is written with the aim of giving practical, down-to-earth, easily understood directions and patterns for the most common biblical characters.

This book is not intended to be an in-depth treatise on historical costumes. It is rather, directed to the amateur costumer of church dramatic presentations with limited financial resources. Designs are based upon both historical and traditional costuming. There are instances in which an authentic design would be so startling or inappropriate, drawing attention to itself, that it would detract immeasurably from the story. (If you doubt that statement, consider at the extreme, the "topless" gowns worn by certain classes of Egyptian and Roman women — hardly acceptable in the most liberal of congregations!)

With planning and preparation, some organization and imagination, all things are possible — even costumes!

Read on!

CHAPTER II:

GETTING SET

Organization

The first step in costuming a biblical play, or any play for that matter, is to select the costumer, the person in charge. This person should be one who is above all, an organizer, for the coordination between the director and those who will do the designing and construction of the costumes is of no small consequence. The costumer will supervise and be responsible for the purchasing, the creation and care of the costumes before and after the show. She (or he) must work carefully with the director so that the production will be a coordinated entity. Each must not go his or her own way.

It is necessary for the costumer to understand the function of the costume. Proper costumes help to establish the time, the mood and the characters in the play. They are able to convey much, both quickly and silently, to the audience. They help the actor to look the part, and hence, feel the part of his or her character. They enhance and reinforce the role.

However, costumes are not the most important part of the production. The story, the message, is uppermost. Everyone involved should understand this. Therefore, the costumer should not allow herself to overestimate the value of her contribution to the production. Costumes are only one element of the production and should be kept in proper perspective. The story, the message, is the primary purpose of biblical drama. Costuming is a tool used to aid the delivery of this message.

After the costumer has been selected (drafted?) and her role established, the next step is to determine what costumes are needed. If your church has some available, undoubtedly stuffed into a carton hidden in the dark recesses of a closet under a stairway, you might count yourself fortunate. But you might be luckier if you have to start from scratch! Some costume collections can be quite ghastly. Or haven't you noticed?

An efficient method of taking inventory of needs is to make a chart. List each character in the production, the costume or costumes he or she will wear, the size, accessories needed, who is responsible for making them, and lastly, a column for checking it off when finished. Make duplicate copies so that each person involved will understand exactly who is responsible for what, and what is needed. The head costumer should keep the master list and be responsible for overseeing each garment and its completion. Enlisting the help of a number of seamstresses will make certain that no one is overburdened. Everyone will then be happier and under less tension. See the sample chart below.

Character	Costume Needed	Size	Accessories Needed	Person Responsible	Completed
Mary	Gown Drape (over head)	32	—	Judy "	
Joseph	Long Robe Overdrape	Med	—	Kay "	
Shepherd I	Long Tunic Aba Headdress	Large	Staff	Jan " "	
Shepherd II	Short Tunic Headdress	Small	Sling	Ruth Jan	
Wise Man I	Robe Crown	Med	Gift	Helen Maggie Carol	
Wise Man II	Robe Crown	Large	Gift	Barb Maggie Carol	
Wise Man III	Robe Crown	Med	Gift	Jean Maggie Carol	

Costume Design

History does not record for us the design of Hebrew apparel. There are, however, ancient drawings and carvings from other nations which include Jewish people. They seem to indicate that the Hebrews adopted the clothing of those among whom they lived, either in their desert wanderings or in captivity.

In choosing the design for each costume, search through books and magazines, church school literature, Christmas cards, etc. Establish a file of pictures which will release a flow of ideas on how to put your costume together. Take notes on colors and construction ideas. Trace pictures from books you can't clip, and make sketches as you watch biblical dramas on television. Remember, stereotyped costumes have been formed in our minds. To some extent, you will want to use these conventional ideas, rather than create a style that will call so much attention to itself that it will detract from the message. The costume will then have failed in its purpose.

Patterns

At least one major pattern company has now developed patterns for the Christmas story. They will be very useful as a springboard for designing your own individual costumes for many biblical characters. There are other appropriate substitutes, however, which are available. A straight or slightly flared long robe or gown pattern is usable. A caftan pattern is very versatile and is available in sizes for men, women and children. A plain blouse pattern with a suitable neckline and sleeves can simply be lengthened and given a flare. If the pattern is one which is opened all the way down the front, place the center front line of the pattern on a fold of the material. *(See Figure 1.)* A simple slit three or four inches down the front of the bodice and tied at the neckline will enable easy slip-on. If possible, cut robes longer than necessary — the next person to wear it might be several inches taller.

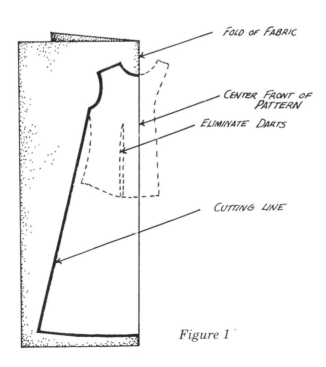

FOLD OF FABRIC

CENTER FRONT OF PATTERN

ELIMINATE DARTS

CUTTING LINE

Figure 1

A sleeved garment constructed by cutting a hole in the center of a length of fabric for the head, and then sewing up the sides is sometimes called a *T-gown* or *T-tunic*. Set-in sleeves were developed after biblical times, so this is the style which would be most commonly used. If the actor wearing a T-tunic is very active on stage, the stitching is apt to pull out so be certain to reinforce the underarm seam.

Don't let the fact that most of the costumes will be made from the same basic pattern worry you. It is entirely probable that ten women may make ten costumes from the same pattern, but all would be different because of the imaginative use of various combinations of colors, additions and trims.

You will also notice as you read through this book, that there are many similarities among the costume styles from one period to another and that the basic form is often the same. This can be a distinct advantage for it allows the costumer to adapt the costumes from one play to the next, thus saving time and expense.

Basic to many nationalities, time periods and classes of people was the versatile tunic. If necessary, it can be modified by changing the type of mantle, accessories and headdress. It can be dressed "up" or "down" to suit different classes of character.

The Hebrew costume changed very little from the Old Testament to the New so that particular change is relatively easy. However, other adaptations can be made. The tunic for Moses could also be used as the base for a Wise Man's outfit. By adding a long, luxurious cape or panel plus fancy pendants, the adaptation is possible, if not the most desirable. The tunic of the shepherd could become the tunica of the Roman soldier by adding the armor. The long tunic made of a fine fabric for Queen Esther can double as the tunic for a well-to-do Roman woman simply by changing the overdrape and headdress. The long tunic of Sarah could double for New Testament women. By adding trims and embroidery it can be used for the upper classes as well as the lower. It is helpful to attach such trims with an easy slip stitch or long sewing machine stitch so they may be quickly removed if needed.

These few examples illustrate how simply adaptations can be made and will stimulate other possibilities as needed.

If your church buys the patterns, stamp each envelope with the church name and file away (bring out the trusty shoe box!) for future use. You can quickly develop a good selection of patterns in both size and style.

Construction

Garments may be speedily sewn together, but should be neatly constructed so that they are presentable even to those in the front rows of the audience. Seams, especially hems, may be made with a long sewing machine stitch so they may be more readily adjusted for a person of a different height. At times, however, a finished edge is not necessary, as costumes are not expected to be judged closely. Indeed, frayed edges and hems are often appropriate for certain classes of characters such as slaves, beggars, shepherds, etc. If a change of clothing must be made quickly, the use of Velcro® for the fastenings will facilitate this.

If it is necessary to lengthen a robe for an actor, and the hem does not allow enough, this may be done by adding a contrasting fabric or trim, such as fringe. A garment may be made wider by using set-in trims or panels.

Finding Materials

Effective costuming does not necessarily require large sums of money. Indeed, proper stewardship of the church's money probably decrees that huge outlays of money are not warranted. For this reason, it is more important than ever to seek and find bargains. Much can be done with items, large and small, picked up for next to nothing at rummage sales or thrift shops. Obviously, you cannot start your search for suitable fabrics the first of November if you are costuming a Christmas play! Begin as early as possible to gather items that might be usable. You will probably purchase a few that won't be used for one play but might be perfect for the next. Also, appeals to church members and friends will often yield great treasures, especially if donors are convinced it is for a great cause. Here is a list of some things to look for:

Bedspreads — *both rough and smooth textured, plain or striped. (Sometimes even a quilted spread is usable.)*

Draperies and curtains — *look especially for one color drapes with woven designs. Some have linings which are also usable.*

Sheets — *also sheet blankets which make a satisfactory substitute for wool.*

Blankets — *if they are fuzzy enough, they might look like an old worn skin and when dyed may be used for shepherds or for John the Baptist. Worn thermal blankets give the textured appearance of hand woven wool. Both striped and plain may be used.*

Remnants — *from the fabric shop. Some designs which do not sell well for modern use are perfect for ancient costumes.*

Samples — *from drapery departments, used for headdresses or panels.*

Bathrobes — *don't leave them looking like bathrobes, however.*

Burlap — *perfect for John the Baptist and other poor classes.*

Scraps — *even small ones for fancy trims on gowns, head-dresses, etc.*

Suede cloth — *for money pouches.*

Felt — *large or small pieces. Heavy industrial weight felt is usable for helmets and as the base for jewelry.*

Flour sacks — *great for headdresses when dyed.*

Formal dresses — *silver or gold ones can be used for trims, panels or turbans.*

Furs — *fake or otherwise. Sheep skin linings are fine for shepherds.*

Scarves

Wide belts — *especially leather-looking ones. Turn the shiny side in and use the rough side.*

Slippers, thongs or loafers.

Bags and pouches for money bags.

Heavy woolen socks.

Hats — *pill boxes, derbies, broad-brimmed, etc.*

Braids, fringe, cording, rope, lace.

Costume jewelry, pendants, chains, rings, bangles, buttons with interesting shapes or designs.

Primitive-looking pottery and urns, baskets, basins for washing feet, gourds for dippers.

Boxes or bottles with interesting shapes — *for the Wise Men's gifts.*

Rams horns — *sometimes found in sporting goods stores.*

Styling

After a good collection of supplies has been obtained, the choice of which fabric to use for which costume must be made and is influenced by several factors. The most apparent is that certain fabrics and colors are associated with specific classes of people. Royalty and aristocracy wore the fabrics and colors which were the most difficult and expensive to produce — the satins, velvets and brocades in the vivid colors of purple and red. The poor, the humble, used the simplest fabrics, coarse, heavy hand-loomed cloth in natural colors. By using these broad designations and the various subtleties in between, the costumer can tell the audience much about the characters in a silent, efficient way.

DYEING CLOTH

No one is fortunate enough to purchase the right piece of fabric with the right color combination for every costume. But most fabrics can be dyed and pleasant and harmonious color combinations can be devised. Fiber glass, from which some draperies are made, is an obvious exception.

When dyeing, consideration must be given to the original color, the fabric content and the pattern or stripe. Read the directions on the dye folder carefully for instructions on how to dye and for advice on which colors to use. The common dyes found in grocery and hardware stores (Rit, Putnam, Tintex, etc.) are union dyes and are best used with the addition of iodized salt. Use one cup of salt to every 8-10 gallons of dye solution.

Boiling water produces the best and most washable coloring, but requires a very large tub and constant stirring. The water in most washing machines is not hot enough and is more properly called tinting. This is easier, however, and by doubling the amount of dye and resetting the timer dial several times to allow at least 30 minutes in the dye bath, satisfactory results are usually achieved. Always clean the machine thoroughly afterward by running the machine through an entire wash cycle using a cup of bleach and several old towels.

Mix the dye powder with boiling water into a paste. Add more boiling water and then strain through an old nylon stocking or several layers of cheesecloth. Try a sample of the fabric in the dye bath first if there is any doubt about the outcome. Also, pay attention to the suggestions given for which color to use over the original color of the fabric to reach the color of your choice. For example, a beige drapery was used to make a shawl for a Wise Man. Yellow dye was used, creating a perfect gold.

It is usually advantageous to make the garment first and then dye it. This is especially true if you are using old sheets. In this way, you will be certain to have enough of the fabric. If you must use part of a second sheet, you can rarely obtain the same color on the second dye-go-round.

Sometimes striped or plaid spreads or draperies can be dyed, producing wonderful results. Brocades or fabrics with self-color designs woven in will dye beautifully with the pattern catching the highlights. The back side of a drapery, if shimmery, will become a magnificent satin for a royal gown. Certain plaids or stripes in spreads or old bathrobes will absorb the dyes in different amounts, creating shades of the same color very effectively.

Special Effects

By all means invest in a can of gold spray paint. It will add a touch of elegance to many articles, especially ornaments and stage props. It may also be used effectively to add highlights to clothing with the use of a finely dispensed spray. Obviously, this must be done with caution, and should be experimented with before using on the finished garment.

Overall fabric designs and borders can be accomplished with linoleum or wood blocks or with stencils. Raised patterns can be created with the use of hot melt glue (applied with a glue gun) and painted later. These patterns must be large enough to be seen beyond the first row of the audience. You cannot think small when it comes to patterns used on stage.

Color shading may be accomplished by spraying with union dyes mixed with water from a spray bottle or with a brush or sponge.

To age fabrics, wash several times. Use a cheese grater, wire brush or rasp to fray edges, hems and elbows, depending upon the degree of wear desired. Spray dyes on fabrics to create a dirty appearance. Paste shoe polish creates a greasy appearance. Spray undiluted bleach on fabrics to fade the color. This may also create holes which might be just the desired effect. However, dacron or nylon blends do not age well.

The use of a heavy layer of paint or heavy starching will make the fabric stiff, which at times might be the exact effect desired. For instance, this is an easy method of producing "armor" for Roman soldiers — spray paint over felt or burlap.

Color is also used on stage to help emphasize a lead character, creating a strong contrast to all the others. As an example, an adult Christ might wear white while those around him would wear darker colors.

Lighting

If strong lighting will be used in the performance, this will influence the choice of colors also. Strong light will fade certain colors, but will highlight others. Satins will reflect light; piled fabrics such as velveteens will absorb light and at the same time denote richness. A drama in the chancel without special lighting will not create these problems, but the combination of color and strong lighting, if used, must be considered and tested long before the dress rehearsal.

Summary

Now you have determined which costumes are needed, what patterns to use and have a supply of materials. Perhaps you have looked at many pictures and have some basic ideas about how to proceed. The following chapters have suggestions which are intended to act as a springboard for your own imaginative talents. Remember that these were created by women with only average artistic ability.

It is hoped that they will spark your own creative abilities, enabling the creation of original costumes, each with its own unique individuality. This is the challenge and the excitement! The fun has just begun!

CHAPTER III:

COSTUMING DESIGNS
(In Approximate Order of Appearance)

Early Hebrew, Chaldean

Some of the Bible's best known stories come from Genesis. The first, with **Adam** and **Eve** as the main characters, would be difficult to visually portray in the local church. It can only be done if the setting gives the appearance of a misty dawn when Adam and Eve are walking through Eden's shrubs and trees, the actors clothed in flesh colored leotards. Indeed, this can be presented very effectively through the harmonious combination of lighting, staging and voice. The effort would not be simple but would certainly be a challenge.

After the Fall and ejection from the Garden, **Adam** and **Eve** are more easily presented. Life for them was primitive and their clothes were simple. They went from garments of fig leaves to garments of skins. These would be the forerunners of the basic tunic, short, perhaps over one shoulder only or perhaps only the skirt. Both should be girded with rope or a narrow, twisted band of cloth.

As time went on and man learned to raise sheep and to weave, his clothing became a little more sophisticated. When **Noah** and his family were upon the scene, their clothing would have been roughly spun wool, or of animal skins. The design would still be the simple tunic, girded with twisted bands of cloth, leather or rope.

For outer wear, they would use a simply draped mantle.

While doing heavy work, the men should wear a simple *loincloth*. This may be made of a rectangular piece of fabric, approximately two feet by two yards, or enough to be wrapped around the body twice, brought from behind, between the legs and tucked into the cloth at the front waist. This will be the standard pattern for the loincloth through all of the biblical plays.

Appropriate colors would be the earth tones — tan, brown, rust, dark mossy green.

Hair should be long, unadorned, except perhaps for a band tied around the brow.

Still in Genesis, **Abram** and **Sarai** appear on the scene. They lived in the land called Chaldea, and here it is that we find the first records of clothing of interest to us. Abram, as other leaders of his time, would wear a straight, long, sleeveless tunic, with fringe at the hemline. His shawl, also fringed, would be cut approximately 50 inches wide and twice the length from the actor's shoulder to the floor. It should be of heavy, but drapable, fabric. An old flannel sheet blanket, dyed an appropriate color, makes a fine shawl. It is worn simply around the shoulders, with each end falling to the floor in front. If spread out upon outstretched arms, Abram's gestures are imposing. He will also wear a leather pillbox hat and leather arm and/or wrist bands.

Abram and other men of this time would be heavily bearded and will be barefoot.

Sarai should wear a long, sleeveless tunic made of a soft fabric, perhaps of an old drapery lining. The tunic may have a narrow decorated border at the neckline, using a simple geometric design. She will also wear a simple cape with a drawstring around the neck. It may be bordered with fringe or a simple design. She also goes barefoot.

Her headdress is a simple drape made of a soft fabric over her hair, falling just below the shoulders. Ankle and arm bracelets complete her costume.

Appropriate colors for Abram and Sarai are dark and strong ones such as rust, brown, indigo, dusky green or ecru.

Later in their lives, when they become **Abraham** and **Sarah** and are traveling and living in the desert, they should don the traditional desert garb. Abraham should wear a long tunic and the aba, as in Figure 22, but it should be of a plain, not striped, fabric. Again the earth tones would be used. He should wear the desert kaffiyeh to keep the desert sands from blowing down his neck. Sarah would wear the same clothing just described, but would add an aba for cooler weather. She might drape her shawl about her head.

The characters of **Isaac, Rebekah, Jacob, Leah, Rachel** and others of this period were also simple people of the land, sheepherders and nomads. Their costumes would be similar to those of Abraham and Sarah. **Esau** probably wore animal skins and as leopards were known during Bible times, an interesting variation would be to have him clothed in such. Imitation leopard skin fabrics are available and could be used for a simple tunic, either the type worn over one shoulder or worn skirt-fashion from the waist to the knee. Sheepskins might also be used.

The women may wear either a sleeveless striped tunic, girded with a wide band, and arm bracelets, or they may wear a fuller, long tunic with very full sleeves. Barefeet or simple sandals are worn. A drape for the head, cut approximately 30 inches by 60 inches, may be worn over the hair, to fall softly behind the shoulders. This style should be fastened to the hair by means of a hidden hat pin so that the actress need not worry about it slipping. As an alternative, this drape may be fastened under the chin, tucking it under the fold at the temple. Either drape may have a simple border or fringe, on the ends.

The same colors as for Abram and Sarai should be used.

The story of **Joseph** presents an interesting costuming possibility. We are familiar with the "coat of many colors" mentioned in the King James version of the Bible for the young boy. However, more recent commentaries state that it was a "coat of extremities," that is, a long coat which reached down to the feet and was made with long sleeves extending beyond the hands. Since the working men generally wore a short, sleeveless tunic, or a loincloth, and Joseph was given this distinctive one in which it would be impossible to work, the roots for extreme jealousy sprang to life rapidly. Also, this type of garment was given to the first born (which Joseph was not), designating him as the heir to the head of the family. In her book, "Joseph," Joyce Landorf envisions his garment as a pure white linen tunic with wide embroidered borders upon the edge of the sleeves and hem. The ornate raised design featured grape clusters

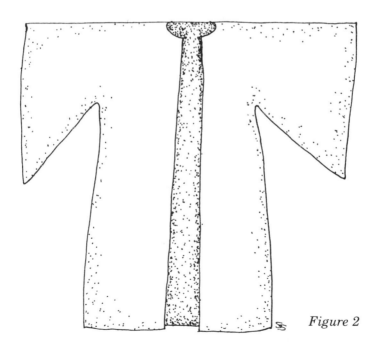

Figure 2

and leaves embroidered with gold threads overlaying many colored threads. However the garment is designed, it should be elegant enough to stir the brothers into their dastardly deed.

The basic cut is that of a T-gown with very long pointed sleeves. *(See Figure 2.)* A fabric with a gorgeous design which can be appliqued upon the robe would make a luxurious costume. If a striped robe is desired, wide, not narrow, stripes of brightly colored fabric may be stitched on. A combination of yellow, deep red, indigo and green would be colorful and appropriate. Underneath this robe, Joseph should wear a short tunic, probably white.

EARLY OLD TESTAMENT HEBREW		
	Males	*Females*
Characters	*Abraham, Isaac, Jacob*	*Sarah, Rebekah, Rachel, Leah*
Style	*Long or short tunic. Aba for warmth. Loin cloth for heavy work scenes.*	*Long, sleeveless tunic, plain or striped. Cape or shawl for warmth. Wide girdle, perhaps lightly decorated.*
Fabrics	*Heavy muslins or linen. Blanket or heavy drapery fabric for aba.*	*Lighter weight muslin, crepe. Flannels, sheet blanket for shawl.*
Colors	*Brown, rust, dusty green, ecru*	*Same. May have light trim at neckline. Fringe at hem of tunic or shawl.*
Hair	*Long. Heavy pointed beard.*	*Long, held back at neck, over ears.*
Head gear	*Kaffiyeh*	*Shawl over head for outdoor wear.*
Footwear	*Barefoot or simple sandals.*	*Same.*
Accessories	*Leather arm or wrist bands. May be studded.*	*Ankle and arm bracelets, simply decorated.*

Egyptian

The Egyptian influence enters the costuming scene after Joseph was captured and transported to Egypt. At the time when the Israelites were in bondage there, clothing for Egyptian nobility was extravagant. Cotton and linen were the fabrics used, and the weave ranged from coarse to extremely fine, even transparent. Decorative effects were created by gold or silver threads woven in, or by patterns woven, painted or embroidered upon the fabric. Colors such as yellow, yellow-green, blue, blue-green, orange-red, deep red and indigo were used. But the predominating color by far was white. Next to the dark skin and black hair, it must have created a striking effect.

The principal garment of the men was a loincloth, a schenti, described previously. Slaves and overseers wore only the loincloth of coarsely woven fabric. Upper-class men wore a loincloth under tightly pleated skirts, which were often transparent. Organdy or batiste would be satisfactory for these sheer skirts. To achieve this pleating, after it has been sewn, dampen it and twist it lengthwise very tightly, and let it dry. If the fabric has no natural stiffness of its own, it may be sprayed with starch before drying. Such a skirt is shown in Figure 3.

With this skirt, the man is wearing a corselet, a vest-type top with hawk feathers across his chest, believed to give him protection. He also wears "apron" tabs attached to his girdle. The tabs were decorated and made of either leather or heavily starched linen. One large panel or three or four smaller ones were worn. **Pharaoh's** apron was jeweled gold.

A standard item of most Egyptian costumes, worn by both men and women, was the large round collar, shown in photograph 1. It was made of various heavy fabrics, felt or leather and decorated with a combination of jewels, beads, shells and/or geometric designs. The collar should be approximately the width of the shoulders, although the higher the rank of the person, the wider the collar should be.

Short pieces of salad macaroni (uncooked, of course) make inexpensive, easy-to-string beads. They may be colored by pouring one to two inches of rubbing alcohol into a jar, adding food coloring and then the macaroni. Shake well and let dry on waxed paper. They can then be sewn or glued onto the collar in combination with felt pieces, braids, "jewels," shells or whatever your imagination dictates.

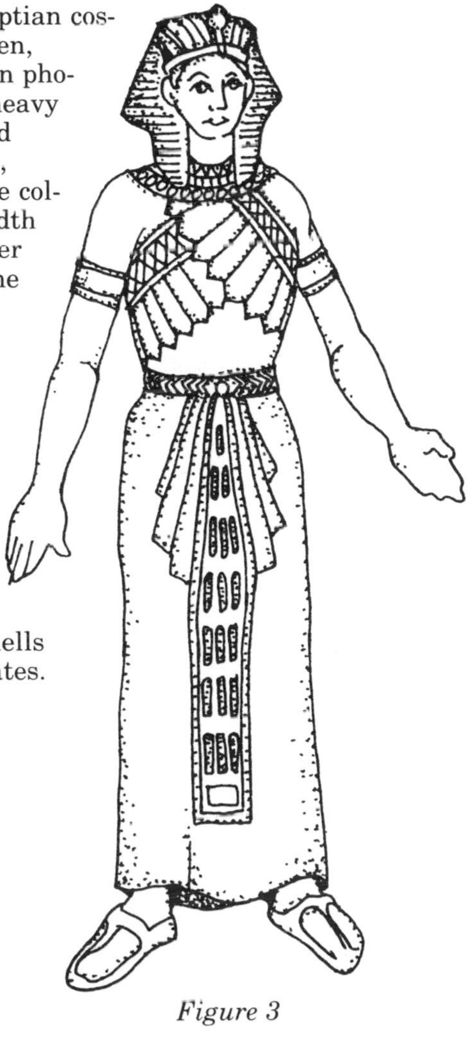

Figure 3

17

The kilt, a short wrap-around skirt, *(Figure 4)* is a second alternative for the Egyptian male. He also wears a girdle, collar and arm and ankle bands. The kilt was often made of striped fabric.

Another style was the long tunic made of soft drapable fabric, girded, and with a collar. This tunic might be accompanied with a long decorated shawl worn over one shoulder and reaching to the floor both front and back. This was held in place by the tunic's girdle.

Yet another style of garment which was used by both men and women was a very full robe. The **princess** in Photograph 1 is wearing this robe. It was made from a rectangular piece of fabric, twice the length of the distance from the shoulder to the floor and as wide as the distance from wrist to wrist when the arms are outstretched. A hole should be cut in the center for the head. The side seams are not stitched together. The front section is pulled toward the back at the waist, and the back is pulled toward the center front. It is held in place with a girdle, belt or fastened with an ornament pin. The round collar is worn with this robe also.

Figure 4

Photograph 1

18

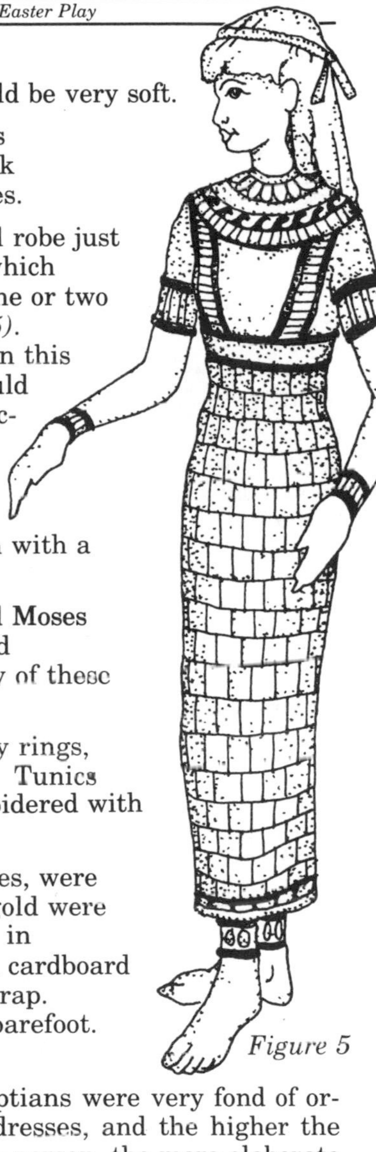

Because of the fullness, the fabric should be very soft.

Pharaoh, Joseph and **Moses** as princes in the court, and other men of rank would have worn any of the above styles.

Women might have worn the full robe just described, or they might wear a skirt which commenced just under the bust, with one or two straps over the shoulders. *(See Figure 5).* Egyptian ladies wore nothing more than this skirt and the round collar, but this would hardly be acceptable in a church production. An alternative would be to add a light, smooth top.

A second costume would have a long, plain or embroidered skirt worn with a round cape and the round collar.

Pharaoh's daughter, who rescued Moses from the bullrushes, her attendants and Potiphar's wife might be dressed in any of these garments.

Both men and women wore many rings, pendants, and arm and ankle bracelets Tunics of the pharaohs were gorgeously embroidered with gold.

Sandals, often with turned-up toes, were worn by the nobility. Bright colors or gold were popular. The sandals worn by Pharaoh in Photograph 1 were made by covering a cardboard sole with fabric and adding a curved strap. However, most often, the people were barefoot. Slaves were always barefoot.

Figure 5

Figure 6

Egyptians were very fond of ornate headdresses, and the higher the rank of the person, the more elaborate the headdress he wore, especially for official occasions. It is suspected, however, that some of the headdresses shown in Egyptian art were never actually worn.

The headdress shown in Figure 6 is the *khat,* the traditional one shown on the sphinx and other carvings. It is made of stiff fabric, usually striped, about 35 by 25 inches. To make the khat, cut a piece of belting or heavy ribbon and staple together forming a

19

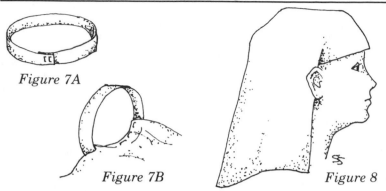

Figure 7A

Figure 7B   *Figure 8*

circle which will fit the wearer's head. *(See Figure 7A.)* Lay the circle in the center along the long edge of the rectangle. Staple the side of one edge to the underside of the circle about halfway around. *(See Figure 7B.)*

Place the band on the head, and bring the material over the top of the head and behind the ears. Take a tuck on each side of the headdress, endeavoring to match the stripes. Pull the front edges of the fabric to the back of the head (underneath the fabric) and fasten with a safety pin. A fold of the material will fall forward. *(See Figure 8.)* Press iron-on pellon between the two thicknesses of the fabric which falls over the front shoulder. This will give body to this portion. Trim the fabric across the back at the shoulder line, as though giving a haircut. Tack gold satin ribbon to the front portion of the headdress, running it toward the back under the front fold. Royalty may add its symbol, the uraeus (asp) at the center front.

The headdress shown on Figure 9 and in the photograph is the mitre of Osiris or Crown of the North, reserved for royalty. Make it from white felt, cut in two pieces, with a cut-out for the ears. Stuff it lightly with polyester fiber. It may be worn plain, trimmed with the uraeus, or as in the photograph 1, trimmed with a red "sun" and two tendrils radiating from it. These are made of felt, strengthened with pipecleaners. The gold feather rising from the sun is also of felt and pipecleaners.

Figure 9

The queen's headdress shown in Figure 10 is the "vulture" headdress, made of gold linen or leather. The vulture is made of gold and jewels.

The headdress in Figure 11 worn by Queen Nefertiti was of red leather, stiffened with buckram. The decorative bands were blue, red, ecru and white.

Other Egyptian women may wear a simple fillet around their brow. Often a perfume cone, filled with fragrant ointment, was worn on top of the head as in Photograph 1. This was made by trimming a styrofoam cone. Lotus blossoms were also frequently worn in their hair.

It was common for both men and women to shave their heads, probably because of the heat and for the cleanliness. In fact, men shaved all of their body hair. Some of the headdresses just described covered the head completely. Wigs were very popular and were created in ornate and stylized fashion. If you have time and patience to try making a wig, begin with a tight-fitting skull cap. Attach lengths of heavy, black rug yarn on the cap, beginning at the lower edge and building layers over it. Trim the ends to create a thick wig. The yarn may be styled in several ways or by braiding. The most simple style would be straight, blunt-cut, and with bangs.

Figure 10

The Hebrews for the most part were slaves in Egypt. Their costumes would be the simple loincloth for the men and straight tunics for the women. Colors, of course, would be drab and the fabric coarsely woven.

Figure 11

21

EGYPTIAN PERIOD		
	Males	*Females*
Class of character	*Nobility*	*Nobility*
Characters	*Prince Moses, Pharaoh, and officials*	*Princess, attendants*
Style	*Loincloth covered by tightly pleated skirt or kilt; decorated "apron", round, wide collar; corselet*	*Loose, full robe with girdle or belt or long skirt with shoulder straps, round collar*
Fabric	*Fine cotton, linen*	*Same*
Colors	*Predominately white; also yellow, yellow-green, blue, blue-green, deep red, orange-red, indigo. Gold trims for the pharaoh*	*Same*
Hair	*Shaved head*	*Shaved head, sometimes with wig*
Head gear	*Ornate headdress, khat*	*Fillet around the head Perfume cone, flowers in hair, ornate headdress for official occasions*
Footwear	*Sandals, some with turned-up toes*	*Same*
Accessories	*Rings, pendants, arm and ankle bracelets*	*Same*

EGYPTIAN PERIOD		
	Males	**Females**
Class of character	Slaves, Hebrews, Moses' family	Same
Style	Loincloth	Long belted tunic
Fabric	Coarsely woven fabrics	Same
Colors	Drab, earth tones	Same
Hair	Long. Bearded.	Long, fastened in back
Head gear	Nothing or headband	Shawl or drape over hair when outdoors
Footwear	Bare feet or simple sandal	Same
Accessories	None	None

Later Old Testament Hebrew

The Israelites left Egypt in great haste, wearing the clothing they had worn as slaves. However, before leaving, they obtained from the Egyptians much gold, jewels and clothing. After the Red Sea crossing, when the tempo of the journey slowed, they might have donned the fancy clothing and jewels they brought with them. As they wearied of their travels, as the desert heat and wind beat upon them, and after they melted their gold to make the golden calf, they must have turned to the nomad garments of Abraham's time. These would be the long tunics, the flowing abas and the kaffiyeh. The stories from the time of **Joshua** would also be costumed in this way.

One additional note: Numbers 15:38 tells us that God instructed Moses (while wandering in the desert) to tell the people to attach tassels on the corners of their garments with a blue cord. This was to remind them to obey the commandments of the Lord and to be holy.

To make a tassel, cut a piece of cardboard slightly longer than the length of tassel desired. Wind yarn round and round this cardboard until desired fullness is achieved. Slip a strand of blue yarn through the entire bundle, leaving the ends to be attached to the garment. Remove cardboard from yarn. Wrap another strand of yarn around tassel, about ½ to ¾ inch down from the head and knot tightly, letting the ends become a part of the tassel. Cut through the opposite end of the bundle of yarn and trim evenly.

God gave to Moses specific directions for the rainment of **Aaron** and subsequent **High Priests** in Exodus 28 and again in Exodus 39. The clothing was to display the glory and beauty of God and was to be used only in God's service in the temple. It was not even to be worn in the Holy of Holies — only linen could be worn there. And

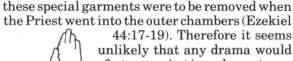

these special garments were to be removed when the Priest went into the outer chambers (Ezekiel 44:17-19). Therefore it seems unlikely that any drama would feature a priest in such a costume, unless it might be after the angel appeared to Zacharias to tell him that Elizabeth, his wife, was to bear a son. He then appeared to the people, making signs to them, perhaps not taking time to change his clothing.

In the event you wish to make the High Priest's costume, be aware of the fact that there are slightly different interpretations of the directions. Also the exact stones and their colors in the breastpiece is uncertain. However, following are the basic instructions. *(See Figure 12.)* First of all, the Priest was to wear a long-sleeved tunic of checker work, probably a woven checked design. Over this he was to wear a blue sleeveless robe of the ephod, reaching to the knees. It was made of one piece, probably woven without seam, with an opening for the head. The bottom edge was embroidered with blue, purple and scarlet pomegranates, and between each pomegranate hung a golden bell.

Figure 12

Over this robe, the ephod was worn. This was a linen garment, cut in two pieces for the front and back, reaching halfway between the waist and the knees. The two pieces were joined at the shoulders, worn with a sash of the same material, and embroidered with threads of gold, blue, purple and scarlet. Two onyx stones, bearing six names of the tribes of Israel on each stone, were fastened upon the shoulders of the ephod. Two chains of pure, twisted gold were attached to golden clasps on the shoulder of the ephod.

A breastplate was worn over this. It was made of a doubled piece of linen, making a pouch. After the folding, it was approximately nine inches square. The linen was of gold, blue, purple and scarlet threads, as for the ephod. Attached to this were four rows of precious stones, set in gold. Upon each stone was the name of one of the tribes of Israel. The first row contained a ruby, topaz (yellow-brown) and emerald; the second row had an emerald, a sapphire and a diamond; the third row, an amber, agate and amethyst; and the fourth, an onyx (black or black and white), beryl (ranging from green, light blue to yellow or pink), and jasper (ranging from red to brown or yellow). Two twisted golden cords were attached to two golden rings on the top edge of the breastpiece and to the onyx stones on the shoulder of the ephod. Two more golden rings were attached to the bottom of the breastpiece with blue ribbons, holding this piece tightly to the ephod.

A mitre was worn upon the head of the High Priest, and upon this was attached, with blue ribbons, a plate of pure gold bearing the words, "Holy to the Lord."

Aaron's sons, and hence other priests, wore long robes and girdles of white. Their mitres were simpler and lower. *(See Figure 13.)*

When the Israelites reached the Promised Land, their neighbors were the Canaanites whose ways were more sophisticated than the newcomers to their land, yet they were still mainly farmers. It was from the Canaanites that the Hebrews learned to weave stripes into their fabrics.

The Philistines also had an influence upon the tribes of Israel at this point, harrassing them with battle after battle. God's people had nothing more than bronze and copper daggers, swords, slings and bows. They had no armor, but probably carried some sort of shield in battle, perhaps of leather. At the same time, the Philistines had iron spears and shields, helmets and coats of mail, and kept their iron-smelting and forging methods secret so that their weapons would remain superior to those of their neighbors.

The working man's garment was still the simple loincloth. A calf-length tunic would be added for other occasions. The colors were usually red, yellow, black, or stripes of these colors. If the men were out in the fields or the desert, they would certainly have worn the kaffiyeh for protection. *(See page 37 for directions for kaffiyeh.)* Otherwise a simple turban was worn.

Animal skins were normally worn only by the poorest people. Woven cloth of wool was common among the herdsmen. Goat hair, brown or black, was used for tent cloth and for clothing for the poor. Mixed with camel's hair, it was very coarse and rough. This was the *sackcloth* worn by mourners through all of the Bible stories.

Gideon, found on the threshing floor by God's angel, would have been wearing a loincloth. Another character, **Samson,** would have worn this simple type of clothing. His wife

Figure 13

and Delilah, both Philistines, would have worn clothing reflecting the Assyrian influence which shall be discussed shortly.

Hebrews had no special nightclothing. Thus when **Samuel** is awakened by the voice of God, and he in turn awakens **Eli,** both would be wearing a simple tunic, ungirded, and probably white.

We have no distinct record of what the judges of this time wore, but scattered pictures indicate that long, straight skirts with fringe at the hemline were worn, with snug, short-sleeved tops. When **Samuel** annointed **Saul** as king, Samuel might have been wearing this costume. Saul, the son of a rich man, would have worn a fine tunic, trimmed with fringe and worn bracelets and necklace. Later, after he lost favor with Samuel and God, we can imagine that his clothing had become more ostentatious, imitating the Assyrian modes.

When Samuel called **David** from his sheep tending duties, David was likely wearing a sheepskin skirt, girded, or a skin worn over one shoulder. He would have been robed in much the same manner when he met the Philistine, Goliath, who would be wearing Assyrian military clothing, described in the next section.

The prophets of the Old Testament would have worn simple clothing of coarse, rough fabric. **Elijah** wore a garment of "hair-cloth," (sackcloth mentioned earlier) with a wide leather belt (II Kings 1:8). He also wore a mantle which he used to strike the waters of the River Jordan, creating a pathway where he could cross. We may assume that other prophets were dressed in similar manner.

Women of this period also wore a simple tunic, ankle length, and usually blue. Embroidery in bright colors, yellow, green, orange and/or red, decorated a square or rectangular area around the front neckline, which was closed with a simple string tie. They, too, would wear some sort of mantle or an aba if near the desert. **Naomi** and **Ruth** may have been dressed in this manner. Ruth, being a Maobite, might have had an Assyrian touch, such as fringe around the hem of her skirt or mantle. Sleeves may also have been long, pointed ones, *(See Figure 2 on page 15)* and the girdle striped or embroidered.

Women of this period and through New Testament times, always covered their heads, to distinguish themselves from the

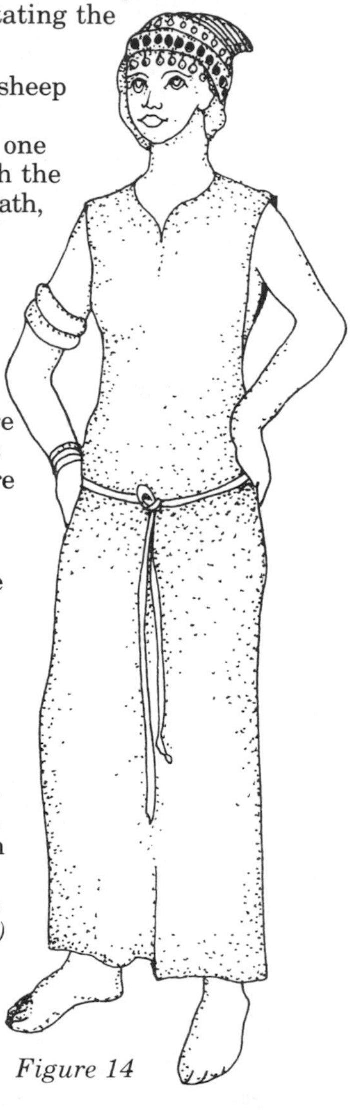

Figure 14

26

prostitutes. Therefore **Rahab** and other prostitutes mentioned in the Bible would not have worn any sort of veil or hair covering. Married women sometimes did their hair in braids and then covered the braids with a cap, something like the dust-cap of a few years ago. This cap was trimmed with a little embroidery and some coins, representing her husband's wealth, hung across the forehead. *(See Figure 14.)* This would be covered with a veil for street wear, the length varying from shoulder length to below the waist. A long veil, edged with embroidery or fringe might be fastened under the chin, covering all the hair.

With the exception of the very poor, women wore much jewelry — beads, bracelets, necklaces, anklets, earrings.

LATER OLD TESTAMENT HEBREW		
	Males	*Females*
Characters	*Joshua, Gideon, Samson, Samuel, Eli, Saul, David*	*Naomi, Ruth, Rahab*
Style	*Loincloth for the working man. Short & long tunics, mantles, wide belts*	*Long tunics, some with long pointed sleeves, embroidery. Striped or embroidered girdle. Mantle or shawl for warmth.*
Fabric	*Wool, flannel, sackcloth*	*Flannel, muslin. Mantle of wool.*
Colors	*Stripes of red, yellow, black. Earth tones, ecru, brown, black*	*Blue, yellow, green, orange, red*
Hair	*Long, pointed beards*	*Braided, fastened around the head*
Head gear	*Kaffiyeh, turban*	*Little cap with embroidery or coin decorations. Veil for street wear*
Footwear	*Sandals or barefoot*	*Sandals or barefoot*
Accessories	*Fringe at the hemline. Bracelets, necklaces.*	*Fringe at the hemline. Beads, bracelets, anklets, necklaces, earrings.*

Assyrian-Babylonian

The Assyrian influence on Hebrew life and costumes runs through approximately half of the Old Testament stories. The Assyrians were a military race, cruel and warlike, their very name striking terror into the hearts of the weaker nations. They conquered the Hebrews and in turn were conquered by the Babylonians. The Hebrews were taken into captivity, and again they adopted the clothing of their conquerors and neighbors. The clothing of the Assyrian and Babylonian civilizations is so similar that they will be treated as one.

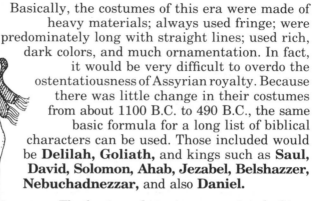

Basically, the costumes of this era were made of heavy materials; always used fringe; were predominately long with straight lines; used rich, dark colors, and much ornamentation. In fact, it would be very difficult to overdo the ostentatiousness of Assyrian royalty. Because there was little change in their costumes from about 1100 B.C. to 490 B.C., the same basic formula for a long list of biblical characters can be used. Those included would be **Delilah, Goliath,** and kings such as **Saul, David, Solomon, Ahab, Jezabel, Belshazzer, Nebuchadnezzar,** and also **Daniel.**

The basic male costume consisted of two garments, a straight tunic edged with fringe, which could be short or long, with or without sleeves, and a fringed shawl. Wool was most commonly used, but at times linen was worn. The tunics of royalty were elaborately embroidered with an all-over rosette design. Embroidered or leather girdles were worn about the waist. The fringe would have been made from two to 20 inches long, and tassels were almost a "must." Colors were bold and brilliant: green, mulberry, indigo, red and yellow. Purple with gold embroidery was reserved for the king.

Figure 15

Lesser characters would also have worn the tunic, but with less ornamentation. Tunics of slaves would have been plain.

The shawls were of various sizes and several methods of draping were used. The one most commonly used for royalty was quite large and the draping was intricate and difficult for the amateur to wear. Therefore, a simpler method, which still appears regal is given here. It is 50 inches by 4½ yards in size, fringed all around with tassels on each corner. One end is draped over the left shoulder, falling almost to the ankle in front. The other end is draped across the back, under the right arm and over the left shoulder to fall towards the floor in back. Careful pleating and draping is necessary and requires time to do it properly. *(See Figure 15.)*

A second royal garment is shown in Figure 16. The basic short sleeved tunic, which should have the all-over rosette design, has 15-16 inch fringe stitched upon it in the pattern indicated in Figure 17. The richness of the colors and the fringe make this elegant also.

A third garment also uses the basic tunic with rosette design. A mantle cut in a long oval, twice the length of the wearer from the shoulder to the knee, and as wide as the distance from shoulder to shoulder. A hole is cut in the center for the head. This mantle is

Figure 16   *Figure 17*

also trimmed with fringe and elegantly embroidered, as is the hem of the tunic.

The all-over rosette design as seen in Photograph 2, may be applied to these robes quite simply. It will take from 75 to 80 circles, two inches in diameter. Mark them on the contrasting fabric with felt tipped pens in the desired colors. Cut them out, plus an equal number of circles from Stitch Witchery®, (placed between rosette and robe) and iron them on. Designs could also be added by lino or wood block or with a stencil.

For daily wear, men would wear an embroidered fillet around the head. Kings and noblemen would wear a tall crowned cap headdress as shown in Figure 15. This may be made from buckram covered with elegant

Photograph 2

cloth. The king's headdress would be embroidered and jeweled, and for official occasions, would be taller. The king's headdress always had a point on the top. Styrofoam may be carved, set on top of the headdress and covered to create this point. Another headdress for royalty would be a tall, straight crown, adorned with a row of feathers around the top and with embroidery. A swath of drapery or ribbons falling from the lower back edge of any of these headdresses would be appropriate.

Horsemen and soldiers wore a knee-length tunic cut up in the front to create an inverted "V", which gave them more freedom of movement. The girdle would be wide leather, held in place by a narrow belt. Soldiers carried their daggers tucked into this belt, or through a short length of chain fastened to the belt. (It was said that the clank of daggers and chain created as the soldier walked was enough to frighten the enemy.) Or he might wear a baldrick, a belt worn diagonally over one shoulder, to carry the dagger or belt. Soldiers might also wear armor *(See section on armor)* and shield, which was usually round. *(See page 69 for directions to make the shield.)* **Goliath** would be dressed in this manner.

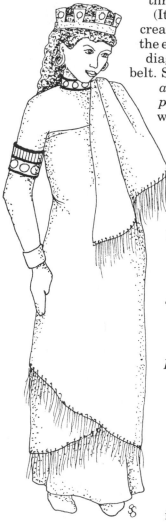

Men wore their hair and beards, which were black, in tight corkscrew curls. Beards were cut straight across. It is possible that wigs were worn. Royalty sometimes sprinkled gold dust in their hair for special occasions!

There are practically no ancient pictures of Assyrian women, but it is believed that their clothing essentially imitated that of the men. The tunic might be long, fringed, short-sleeved, with a round neckline. About the neck, royal women would wear a jeweled "dog collar." Shawls may be draped in several ways, imitating those of men. If an Assyrian woman is to be in public, as she rarely was, she must have her shawl over her head. *(See Figure 18.)*

Women wore a fillet or coronet on their heads. The coronet may be made of gold poster-board, and then trimmed.

As with men, their hair was also long, and tightly curled. Both men and women wore an excess of heavy earrings, necklaces, bracelets and armbands.

Fringe, in the quantities used for Assyrians, is expensive to buy. There are substitutes which can be tried. One suggestion is to cut fringe

Figure 18

from strips of felt. Another, which should only be used if the audience does not sit too close to the actors, is to tear fringe from long strips of sheeting, dyed to the proper color. With both the felt and the sheet fringe, a double layer would be helpful. These alternatives, of course, are not as satisfactory as actual fringe.

Assyrians, both men and women, often went barefoot. Otherwise sandals were worn. Hunters wore high boots to the knee, bound with leather thongs. A substitute for boots may be made by painting or dyeing heavy woolen socks.

ASSYRIAN — BABYLONIAN		
	Male	*Female*
Class of characters	Nobility, royalty	Same
Characters	Goliath, Saul, David, Solomon, Ahab, Belshazzar, Nebuchadnezzar, Daniel	Delilah, Jezebel
Style	Straight tunic, long or short, with or without sleeves and a fringed shawl with tassels. Embroidery for royalty. Embroidered or leather girdles.	Long, fringed tunic, short-sleeves, round neckline plus fringed shawl.
Fabric	Heavy fabrics, sometimes linen.	Same
Colors	Brilliant — green, mulberry, indigo, red and yellow. Purple with gold embroidery for royalty.	Same
Hair	Black, cork-screw curls. Beards curly, cut straight across	Long, tightly curled
Head gear	Embroidered fillet around head for daily wear. Tall crowned headdress for special occasions.	Fillet or coronet
Footwear	Barefoot or light sandals	Barefoot or light sandals
Accessories	Heavy earrings, necklaces, bracelets and arm bands.	Jeweled "dog collar," earrings, bracelets, and arm bands.

31

Persian, Mede

In comparison to the Assyrian modes, the Persian was far more subdued. Persians continued to use the tunic and shawl, but introduced, to these civilizations, at least, the coat with set-in sleeves and the trousers.

The most important garment to be used in biblical dramas was the *candys*. Kings such as **Cyrus, Darius** and **Ahasuerus** would have worn this robe. Their noblemen and officials would have worn the same style, though theirs would not be as elaborate. The candys was made of a rectangular piece, twice the height of the actor and as wide as the distance from wrist to wrist when the arms are outstretched. A sidewise oval for the head is cut in the very center of this rectangle, and the sides are seamed up from the bottom, leaving a 20-inch space for the arms at the top. A girdle, silver or gold for the king, is worn around the waist to blouse the fabric, especially at the sides where it must be higher than at the centers for mobility of the arms. *(See Figure 19 and Photograph 2.)*The king's candys was bluish purple, ornamented with silver or gold. Lesser dignitaries wore red.

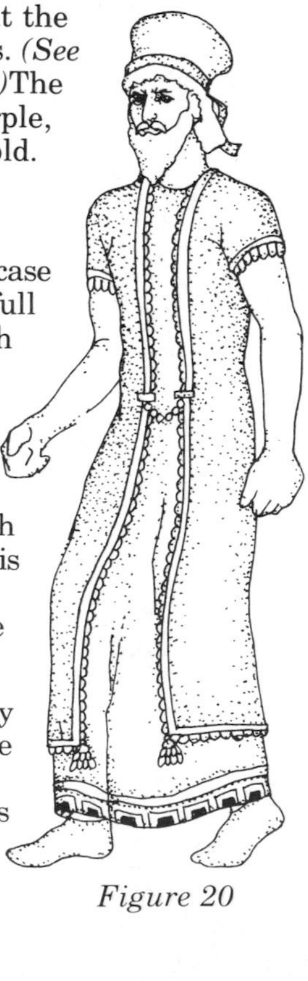

Figure 19

Trousers, as mentioned before, were worn beneath this robe, to peek below the hem. In the case of the king in the photograph, he is not wearing full trousers — just short leggings of gold fabric, which unfortunately, do not show.

Officials such as **Haman,** and **Mordecai** after he was appointed Prime Minister, would wear the garment as seen in Figure 20. Or they could also be costumed in a knee-length tunic with long trousers, topped with the long-sleeved coat. This coat should be lapel-less and be banded around the edges with embroidered borders, or with fringe. The tunic should be trimmed in the same manner.

The headdress shown is made of felt and may be made by covering a pillbox hat and trimming the edge with an inch-wide ribbon, letting the ends hang down in the back. Some costumers and display houses have inexpensive plastic derbies which could be used. The brim should be cut off and the form built up and forward slightly with polyester fiber before

Figure 20

covering.

When Mordecai went into mourning, he would have worn a simple, dark tunic of sackcloth and would have tousled hair.

The king's crown shown in Photograph 2 was made of gilt posterboard and decorated with gold seals and large sequins. The top edge is created with folded pipecleaners glued to the inside top of the crown, with large sequins decorating the peaks. It might have been made of double strength buckram covered with gold cloth and then ornamented.

The scepter which the king is holding was made from a gilded dowel. The knob is the bottom portion of a foam Christmas tree. A tassel decorates the other end.

The hair of the Persians was worn long and curly. Moustaches were always worn; beards were pointed.

Men as well as the women, wore jewelry. Favorites were large hoop earrings, gold collars and chains, and the decorated "dog collars". Men often carried a straight staff or cane with a knob on the top.

Barefeet were common, but shoes, if worn, were usually of yellow leather and covered the entire foot and ankle, fastened by straps.

Persian and Assyrian women were rarely seen in public, but a queen such as **Esther** might appear in several scenes from Old Testament dramas. She would wear a belted, straight tunic with fringe at the hemline and a fringed scarf approximately 15 inches wide by five yards in length. The scarf is draped by permitting it to hang down the front from the right shoulder to the knee. It is then draped across the back, under the left arm, diagonally across the bodice and finally allowed to fall over the right shoulder toward the floor in the back. Care must be taken to keep the folds straight and the fringe in view as much as possible. *(See Photograph 2.)* Esther would also wear a jeweled "dog collar".

Her headdress would be crown-shaped, jeweled, and festooned with a gauze veil falling from the crown down to her waist. Her hair is parted down the middle and drawn to the back of the head, there to be hidden by the veil.

It is believed that Persian royalty often wore a purple ribbon streaked with white around the head, and this may have been the type of "crown" which Ahasuerus placed on Esther's head. This crown may be made by using a wide satin ribbon, stitched onto belting to keep it stiff, the ends of the ribbon allowed to hang down the back.

Fabrics for Persian garments were woolens, heavy linen and leather. These may be substituted with heavy muslin, sateen, outing flannel and imitation leather.

Suggested colors are those which the Assyrians used, plus soft yellow, yellow-green and vivid turquoise.

PERSIAN — MEDE		
	Male	**Female**
Class of character	Royalty, dignitaries	Same
Characters	Cyrus, Darius Ahasuerus, Haman, Mordecai	Esther, attendants
Style	Candys, tunics, robes. Trousers underneath.	Straight, fringed tunic. Girdle at waist. Long fringed shawl.
Fabric	Woolens, heavy linen, leather. Candys from soft, drapable material.	Same
Colors	Red for dignitaries. Bluish-purple with gold ornamentation for the king.	Soft yellow, yellow-green, vivid turquoise
Hair	Long and curly. Pointed beards.	Long, parted in the middle, drawn to the back.
Head gear	Headdress. Crown for king.	Fillet about the brow. Crown-shaped headdress, jeweled, with gauze veil for special occasions.
Footwear	Barefoot, or yellow leather ankle-high shoes	Jeweled sandals
Accessories	Girdle, silver or gold for the king. Staff or cane with knob on top. Jewelry, earrings, jeweled "dog collar".	Jeweled "dog collar", earrings.

Christmas

Angel

The Angel of the Annunciation is often portrayed as female, but Luke gives him the name of Gabriel, a male name. In fact, most angels appearing in the Scriptures seem to have been asexual or male, so do not discard that idea. No matter which sex is used, the most appropriate costume for an angel, if visual, is a long, flowing gown. A white sheet will work for the fabric, but if you can find or afford a more gossamer fabric, it will greatly contribute to an ethereal effect.

Forget about tinsel attached to the gown, even for the little cherubs, and forget about wings. It is much too difficult to construct wings that are in proportion to an adult body and to strap them on firmly enough to keep them secure, yet allow freedom of movement. A wing-like illusion may be created with long, full sleeves or with half-circles of sheer fabric stitched from the shoulder seam down the full length of the long sleeve. *(See Photograph 3.)* A unique opportunity is afforded the lighting "engineer" here to create a spirit-like quality surrounding the angel's appearance. Experiment with the soft lights coming from behind the angel, or with a spotlight from above.

If a *halo* is desired, and you may wish to dispense with it if a male angel is used, it may be made from a circle of silver foil cardboard, 12" in diameter. Cut out an inner circle 6" in diameter, making it 1½" from the lower edge. Finally, attach a small piece of comb to the upper and lower edges of the inside circle to hold it in place. Another style of halo which is more easily secured to the hair is the one shown in Figure 21. It also must be worn on the back of the head, with the flanges secured with bobby pins.

Mary

Mary's costume will be relatively simple, the basic part being a long, straight gown that may have long or short sleeves. It seems quite traditional that Mary's color is blue and two shades of this color make a pleasing

Photograph 3

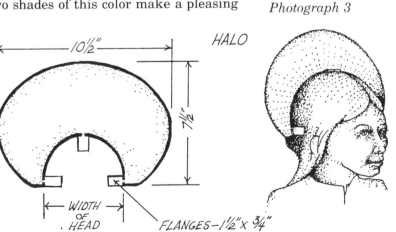

HALO

10½"

7½"

WIDTH
OF
HEAD

FLANGES—1½"X ¾"

Figure 21

combination. The girdle and drape might be of a lighter or darker shade of blue than that of her gown, which might have simple embroidery around the neckline and sleeve edges. Her overdrape is worn in the same manner as Joseph's (described later), but is draped over her head and then allowed to fall down the front. However, for more freedom of movement, she may wear a separate

headdress that is folded in layers above her brow, drawn down to cover her ears and then tied underneath her hair in back. This head covering should be of a softly folding fabric and should be at least 30 to 40 inches square. Tapes sewn to the edge of the drape are more easily tied than the fabric. Arrange this drape so that little, if any, hair is displayed. *(See Photograph 4.)* Mary will also wear sandals.

Photograph 4

Joseph

The basic garment for Joseph and most of the male characters is a long sleeved, ankle-length tunic. It could have a V-neck or a round neckline with a slash down the front, tied with strings.

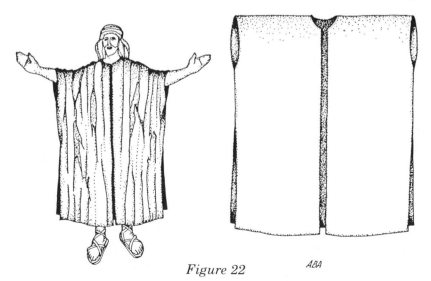

Figure 22

ABA

A wide girdle or band of fabric tied around the waist is also worn. *(See Photograph 4.)*

Over this, Joseph might wear the *aba*, which had been a basic part of the desert dwellers clothing for generations, and was worn for warmth and protection from harsh winds. This can be made from a straight length of fabric, using the full width. *(See Figure 22.)* A striped fabric would be suitable for Joseph. However, if the scene is not out of doors when he would have needed the aba for warmth, Joseph might wear an *overdrape*. This should be made of a fabric which will lie softly in folds and should be at least four yards long.

There are several ways to drape Joseph, but a simple way is to fasten the fabric securely at one shoulder, allowing approximately 20 to 30 inches to fall down the back. Drape the longer section across the chest, under the arm, across the back and over the shoulder to hang down the front. *(See Figure 23.)* Fasten securely so the actor need not worry about losing it. (Hebrews didn't have safety pins but they are a helpful tool for the costumer if they can be hidden.) Joseph's overdrape might be a two or three tone stripe which picks up the basic color of the tunic. Good colors would be varying shades of blue, green or rust.

Joseph would wear a *kaffiyeh* or headdress, a piece of cloth at least 30" square. It should be of a soft fabric, dyed an earthy color. Old dishtowels or linings are very satisfactory. It is folded into an uneven triangle, worn on the head with the folded edge just above the eyebrows and held in place with another strip of fabric or cord tied around the head. This strip is sometimes twisted into a rope-like band.

Figure 23

Innkeeper and Wife

The innkeeper also will wear the basic tunic. To add a little variety, however, he might wear a wide girdle in place of the overdrape. It should be at least 4" wide and of a bright color or imitation leather. If he is a well-to-do innkeeper, he might wear an ornamented collar or neckpiece. He also will wear a headdress.

The innkeeper's wife, also probably a notch or two above Joseph and Mary on the economic scale, might wear a gown a little more elaborate than that of the Virgin. She would not need a cloak unless the play action takes her out-of-doors. Her dress might have embroidery around the neckline, sleeves and sash. Her headdress would be like the tied version for Mary. Suggested colors would be orange or rust.

Shepherds

In all probability, the shepherds were very poor and would be dressed simply and in roughly textured, possibly tattered clothing. As with Joseph, their basic garment would be the tunic, knee-length for the younger shepherds. They would also wear a girdle, or perhaps a piece of rope, around their waists.

Variations can be made in several ways. One shepherd could wear the aba, described previously. Heavy, rough materials would be suitable, such as might be found in draperies or bedspreads. A worn thermal blanket, with the satin bindings removed, has a hand-loomed appearance. These should be dyed in dark, earthy colors or perhaps dark blues or greens.

Another shepherd might wear a knee-length, sleeveless tunic over the long tunic. Still another might have a folded blanket draped across one shoulder, held in place with fabric tied about the waist. Or the blanket could be draped over the head and around the shoulders. If you are fortunate enough to find some sheepskin, even fake, it could be used to make a vest, tied in the front with a leather thong.

Shepherds will wear a headdress and sandals, although younger shepherds might go bare-headed and barefoot.

In Photograph 5, the shepherd holding the staff is wearing the aba made from an old bedspread. The shepherd holding the lamb wears a heavy overdrape from a brown bedspread. The shepherd

Photograph 5

kneeling on the right wears a sleeveless, belted vest over his long tunic.

Wise Men

The Wise Men's costumes are by far the most challenging and gratifying to create. Their dramatic effect is limited only by the imagination of the costumer. It is in this area where the searches through rummage sales and thrift shops will reap satisfying dividends.

Traditionally the Wise Men came from different countries, so their clothing will be a dramatic contrast from the Hebrew clothing and may even vary from one another. They might have a Persian, Oriental or African flavor. Basically, however, each costume would consist of a long tunic with some sort of cloak, train or drape. A basic caftan pattern will suffice nicely for the tunic and lends itself easily to added variations. Choose the richest looking fabrics you can locate. The brocades, velveteens and satins are your choicest selections. Perhaps you have found a velveteen skirt or jumper. It may be lengthened by using a top or straps of muslin, adjustable if possible for varying heights of actors. The fabric available might limit you somewhat in design, but by using ingenuity many problems can be

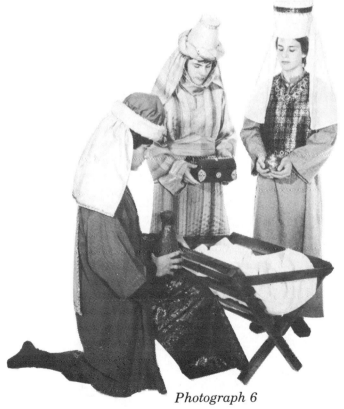

Photograph 6

overcome. For instance, the skirt, sleeves and neckline might be made of the elegant fabric and the body portion which will be covered by an addition of a cloak, train or drape, may be constructed of an old sheet. Scraps of the good fabric should be saved for trims on the crown, thus tying the various parts of the costume into one entity. Even a narrow waistband can be used for a band around the crown.

The costumes in Photograph 6 are as follows:

The kneeling Wise Man wears a long red and gold tunic constructed from cotton "house coat" fabric, to which a loose red cloak, formerly a ribbed bedspread, was added. A gold panel edged with gold sequins and a beaded band hangs down the back. His crown is constructed by placing a cone made of poster board over the top of a woman's hat, and layering fiber-fill around this cone. It is covered with a circle of fabric, gathered around the edge and drawn up to fit over the cone. A long tube of fabric, 3" wide and stuffed lightly with fiber-fill is tacked around the edge. A flowing scarf of gold fabric, edges trimmed with gold sequins, hangs down the back. "Jewels" adorn the front of the band. *(See Figure 24.)*

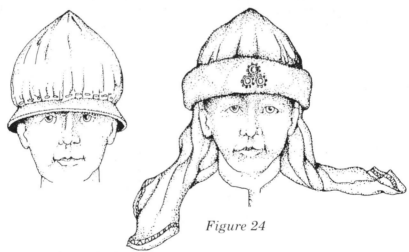

Figure 24

The Wise Man in the center *(Photograph 6)* wears a long tunic constructed of drapery fabric, dyed gold, and turned wrong-side-out to display the satiny side. Over this is a long "vest" constructed of the quilted portion of a bedspread and a fringed shawl (not visible) made from a brocade drapery swag, also gold. The wide girdle and trim on the crown are made from the flounce portion of the quilted bedspread, thus utilizing their harmonious colors.

His crown is fez-shaped, the base being constructed of poster board and attached to the foundation of a woman's hat. It is covered with gold drapery material. Two long tubes of the bedspread flounce material, 2½" in width and stuffed lightly with fiber-fill, are twisted loosely and fastened at the base of the crown. Additional fabric is wound around the head and fastened at the base of the neck, completely covering the ears. The drape down the back is also constructed of flounce material. *(See Figure 25.)* It is presumed that these bindings and scarves were protection from desert sand and wind.

Figure 25

The tunic for the Wise Man on the right *(Photograph 6)* is made of a brocade drapery dyed purple. As there was not enough fabric, the waist portion was made of a sheet dyed purple at the same time. The short vest was made from a colorful, long formal skirt, trimmed with gilded gaskets and woman's belts. The crown form is an upside down lampshade, covered with silver fabric from a woman's formal dress, trimmed with a band of the vest material with small sized gilded gaskets. The scarf which flows down the back of the crown is of a lavender, gossamer fabric (nylon curtain fabric). It was dyed with the drapery panel for the gown and did not accept the same amount of pigment, thereby creating a lovely harmonious combination. *(See Figure 26.)*

Figure 26

The costumes worn in photograph 6 were made very quickly from easily acquired materials, illustrating what can be accomplished with a minimum of time and expense. More elaborate costumes and headdresses can be constructed by anyone with time, interest and a minimum of talent.

Following is a list of other suggestions which might be used.

1. Add a long train constructed from a fringed drapery panel, fastened at the shoulders or in the front with a "jeweled" brooch. *(See section on jewelry.)*

2. Make a full, white robe with wide embroiderd bands criss-crossed over the chest. Add a white turban with embroidered bands.

3. Add a free flowing panel down the front and/or back of a tunic. A metallic fabric makes a fine background. Net or fine lace, spray-painted gold before attaching to the foundation, gives the appearance of an expensive fabric.

4. Use the pattern of brocade fabric as the basis of a design in the tunic or panel.

5. Stencil designs on the fabric with templates or lino blocks.

6. Appliqué strips of velvet or fur on the sleeves and hem of the tunic.

7. Use suggestions from the section on Persian costumes. There is a possibility that a Wise Man came from that area.

8. Use an old hat as the base for a crown, padded and covered. Construct an ornately shaped crown of heavy gold foil around the rim. Or add a ring of "ermine" around the base of the crown. Ermine can be fabricated from white fake fur, dotted with ink or a black felt pen.

9. Use chicken wire to create forms not possible with the above methods. It is easily squeezed here and there, bent, clipped and rearranged. It must be padded well before finishing, both for comfort and for hiding the wire pattern.

Footwear for the kings can be more of a problem than for other characters. Men with small feet might be able to find a woman's gold scuff or slipper which would fit. Or an old pair of slippers might be spray-painted with gold or a harmonizing color. If the shoe situation becomes desperate, black stockings would be less noticeable than inappropriate shoes. *(See also the section on footwear.)*

CHRISTMAS		
	Male	**Female**
Characters	Joseph, Innkeeper, etc.	Mary, Innkeeper's wife
Style	Long sleeved, long tunic, wide girdle. Plus aba or overdrape.	Long, straight gown, belted. Overdrape. Could be embroidered.
Fabric	Medium to heavy, wool or flannel.	Muslins, flannel
Colors	Brown, rust, dark green, stripes.	Blue, orange, rust
Hair	Long, mostly covered with kaffiyeh.	Long, drawn to the back. Covered with veil for out of doors.
Head gear	Kaffiyeh	Cap and/or shawl
Footwear	Sandals	Sandals
Accessories	None, except as play directs.	None, except as play directs.

CHRISTMAS		
	Shepherds	**Wise Men**
Style	Long or short tunic, aba, overdrape, ragged, soiled in appearance. Girdle or rope at waist.	Long tunic or gown. Luxurious cape, shawl or robe. Embroidered or fancy girdle.
Fabric	Heavy, rough fabrics, sheepskin. Should not look new.	Brocade, velvet, satin, fur
Colors	Earth tones, black, ecru, dark blue or green. Some stripes.	Purple, red, indigo, white, gold
Hair	Long or short, curly or straight, tousled, bearded or clean-shaven.	Long, if not hidden. May be bearded or not.
Head gear	Kaffiyeh, wide headbands, overdrapes covering head.	Crowns, turbans, some with veils
Footwear	Rough sandals or barefoot. Leggings fastened with rope.	Sandals or leather shoes, jeweled or ornamented.
Accessories	Shepherds staff, sling	Jewels, necklaces, pendants, plus gifts for the Christ child.

EASTER

The garments of **Jesus Christ,** the main character of the Easter drama, are described in the Scriptures. As with Jewish men at that time, he wore a robe, girdle, headpiece, sandals and the tunic, which for Jesus at this time was the kolobian, woven without seam from top to bottom. In addition, he was draped with a purple robe after his scourging and given a crown of thorns.

Jesus should wear off-white for dramatic effect and emphasis. It might be possible to find jersey tubing or perhaps pillowcase tubing which will fit your particular actor. If not, make the seams vertical and as invisible as possible. There should be slits at the center top of the head and at either side for arms. This should be girded, perhaps with a wide, rich blue band doubled around the waist. Over this Jesus should wear a white, full sleeved aba. A simple white headdress and sandals complete his costume.

The purple robe which was placed upon him by the taunting Roman soldiers was probably an overdrape as described previously. This color, reserved for royalty, ranged in color from a deep scarlet to a mulberry color.

The *crown of thorns* presents a problem. Barbed wire could be used, winding strands around the head several times, if the barbs can be removed or cut on the inner side. Or two-stranded wire could be wound around in the same manner, with nails poked to the outside through the strands. However it is done, the crown must look cruel and stark without actually puncturing the actor.

Short hair on this actor might disturb the over-all traditional effect. It might be wise to rent an appropriate wig for Jesus to wear, but great care must be made to insure that it is one of quality and realism. It is imperative that this representation is believable and sincere.

The disciples and other Jewish men, including **Simon of Cyrene,** will wear basically the same type of clothing. There must be some variety and distinguishing touches however. Changes may be made in the tunics — some short, some long, some ragged. Abas and overdrapes may be used while some men may go without a mantle of any kind. The headdress might be varied with kaffiyehs and turban-type head coverings, and some men might go bareheaded. Suitable colors are brown, gray, wine-red, dark blue, ochre and dusky green with touches of yellow or orange.

The garments of the priests which were described specifically in Exodus 28 as commanded by God, were for wear while performing their temple duties. The Scriptures say that the priests were to put on other garments when leaving, but what they were to wear is not described. Tradition generally pictures them wearing the long white, girded tunic. Sometimes a long-sleeved, full robe of a darker color is added. A mitre or a headdress the same color as the robe might be worn. This is made from a rectangular piece of fabric draped over

the head, bound by several wrappings of fabric, or is worn over a small skull cap. In this case, it would be necessary to use an old-fashioned hat pin to hold the drape in place. The prayer shawl may be worn around the shoulders or may replace the dark drape over the head. It may also be folded into a triangle and tied about the waist. The prayer shawl is of an off-white color, with narrow dark stripes woven in. The Lord also prescribed tassels to be upon the four corners, attached by cords of blue. (Numbers 15:38) The scribes and Pharisees of New Testament times were known for their extra long tassels. *(See Figures 13 and 27.)*

Figure 27

In the scene which involves the hastily convened court for the trial of Jesus, variety may be lent to the costumes by having each of these methods used. These costumes would be worn by **Caiphas, Annas,** the Pharisees, scribes and other members of the Sanhedrin, and **Joseph of Arimathea.**

Herod was the Jewish ruler of Galilee, but was ambitious and pro-Roman, not at all pious. He can be expected to wear luxurious clothing. A basic long tunic with gold trimming or jewelry around the neckline and a rich-looking robe and golden girdle should make him look pompous enough. *(See Photograph 7.)* Suitable colors for him might be rich green, deep red or royal blue. Herod might also be wearing a fez or headdress resembling a crown made of the same fabric as his robe. A tassel or ornamental buttons studding the rim will complete the head gear.

Herod might also wear a heavy necklace and other jewelry. The necklace shown in the photograph was made of a thin piece of styrofoam, gilded and decorated with beads, sequins and bangles. *(See also the section on jewelry.)*

Barabbas had been a member of the rabble. At this point in the Easter story, if he appears, he will have just been released from prison. Surely he would emerge no better dressed than when he had been arrested. A grimy, ragged tunic, perhaps made of burlap or other coarse fabric and girded with a rope or twisted

Photograph 7

length of cloth would be suitable.

The Scriptures relate that many women were present at the crucifixion and resurrection. It is appropriate for them to be clothed in somber tunics, robes and veils covering their heads. These dark colors help set the tone of grief and despair.

A Roman official, such as **Pilate,** should be dressed in the *tunica* and *toga,* the toga being a garment reserved for Roman citizens only. The tunica which would be appropriate for him would be white, short-sleeved and knee-length. It would have a two-inch wide purple band down the center front and back. His toga would have a six-inch wide purple band around the curved edge. Since the toga was normally woolen, a heavier fabric would be needed than for the tunica. Flannel sheet blankets make an acceptable substitute for wool. The dimensions should be 16 to 18 feet along the straight edge and six feet at the widest part of the arc. *(See Figure 28.)*

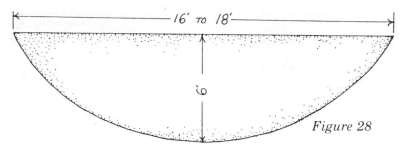

Figure 28

Proper draping of the toga (and the Greek himation) is extremely important. For the toga, one end of the semi-circle is allowed to fall from the left shoulder, down the front of the body to the left foot, with the straight edge next to the throat and the curved edge toward the hand. For the himation, one corner of the large rectangle falls to the left foot with the longer edge next to the throat. The following directions apply to both the mantles.

Approximately half of the fabric is gathered in soft folds on the shoulder with enough remaining to reach almost to the wrist. The left arm should be held outstretched to hold the folds in place. The straight edge of the toga is then draped across the back to the right hip, keeping the folds smoothly in place, brought under the right arm and across the chest to the left shoulder once more, keeping the border as smooth and visible as possible. Again, most of the fabric is draped in folds on the shoulder, with the remainder laid smoothly upon the left arm which should still be outstretched. The end of the toga is then allowed to fall from the shoulder to the floor in back.

For variety, the last step may be changed by draping the toga or himation across the left forearm instead of being carried up to the left shoulder.

The fullness must be carefully arranged to drape in neat

"pleats," to cover the legs in back and not drag on the floor. It is helpful to use safety pins at strategic points and perhaps to tuck the toga under the girdle at several places to hold it in place. The actor must also use his left hand and arm to hold it properly. This is a very imposing garment and will take the actor practice to wear it with dignity. It also takes practice, and perhaps an extra pair of hands, to drape it properly.

However, since Pilate had been a military man and was in charge of military affairs in Judea, you might choose to costume him in Roman military costume.

A relatively easy-to-make outfit for a **Roman soldier,** as pictured in Photograph 7, consists first of all of the tunica, rust in color. Over this he wears the cuirass, a piece of armor consisting of a breastplate and backplate. This was made of felt, spray-painted several times for stiffness with bronze-colored paint. In Roman times, this was hinged on one side and fastened with straps on the other. In place of the hinge in this case, both sides were fastened with straps and buckles, making it adjustable for different actors. Fastened to the bottom of the cuirass is a leather (vinyl) waistband and the hanging leather straps. These are ornamented with cap bolts from the hardware store, glued on with a "super" glue. At the shoulders of the cuirass are wide leather bands connecting the back and front sections of the armor. These are tacked in place except for one end which has Velcro® for ease in slipping on. Attached to these bands are shorter straps, also decorated with the cap bolts. A plastic Roman short sword and sheath from the toy store is fastened to the waistband. A handyman could also make a sword, as pictured in the section on Properties.

The helmet is made from a bump hat, sprayed with bronze paint. Attached to the inside of the helmet are the neck and forehead flaps and the chin straps. Two leather straps, 1½ inches wide, cross over the top of the helmet and a hook is screwed through the center. This helmet was worn by the regular soldiers.

A **centurian** would wear the captain's helmet as in Figure 29. The base for this helmet is a child's football or baseball helmet. The visor and neck guard are cut from acrylic plastic, heated to create the desired form, and attached to the base with pop rivets. A good quality vinyl floor covering may also be tried but would not be as durable. A centurian would add a red plume at the front.

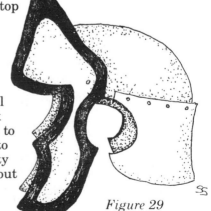

Figure 29

A more elaborate helmet may be constructed with chicken wire in the manner of figure 30 A and B and then covered with felt. Two layers of industrial felt are needed to hide the chicken wire framework. Soak the felt with a mixture of two parts white flexible glue to one part water. Stretch and smooth the felt to fit the form. Let dry between layers. Paint inside and out and decorate as desired. If the horsehair fan on the top of the helmet is desired, a flanged cardboard framework may be glued upon the top of the helmet and the "horsehair" fastened to this support. A reasonable substitute for stage wear may be made of several thicknesses of red fringed felt or many pieces of red pipe cleaners or chenille.

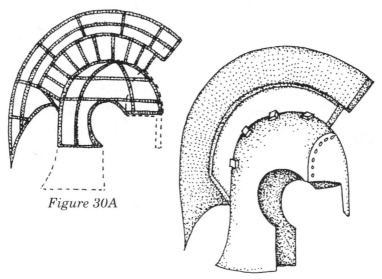

Figure 30A

Figure 30B

The soldier in the photograph is wearing only sandals as he is not in battle. Otherwise, he could wear shin guards constructed from imitation leather, laced up the back with leather thongs. *(See figure 31).* Or the soldier may wear breeches with thongs wrapped around the calves. *(Also see the section on Footwear.)*

Greek

The next major influence upon biblical costuming comes from Greece, appearing in stories which occur in New Testament times. Greeks were numbered among the followers of Jesus; young **Timothy** was the son of a Greek father and would apt to be dressed in Greek fashion, at least in his youth; and **Lydia,** merchant of purple cloth and convert of Paul, who opened her home to missionaries. There were also Greeks whom Paul encountered in Athens when he delivered

Figure 31

his famous "Unknown God" speech. Consequently, nearly every crowd scene would have actors in Greek costume.

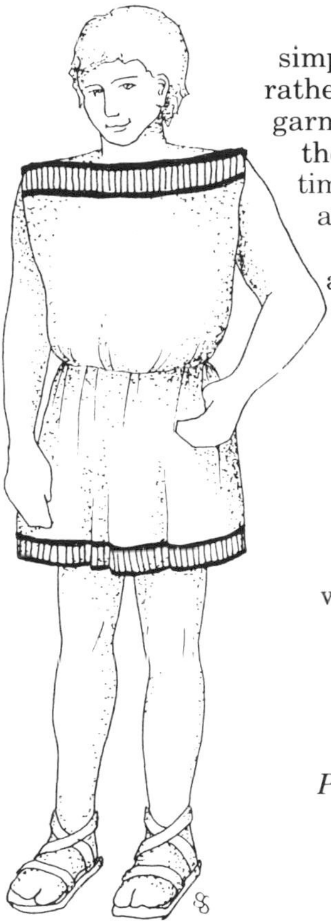

The garments of the Greeks were known for their simplicity, their beauty due to the graceful draping rather than elaborate design and trimmings. The basic garment, for both men and women, young and old, was the tunic known as the *chiton*. In New Testament times, the Ionic style chiton was being used. It varied as to length, the width which formed the sleeve, the girdling and the trim. Young men, boys, peasants and slaves wore a short sleeveless chiton. The back and front pieces were cut as wide as the distance from elbow to elbow with the arms outstretched, and as long as the distance from the shoulder to the knee, plus two inches for blousing. The right side seam was stitched, leaving approximately 10 inches for the arm at the top. Greeks left the left side unstitched, but your actors will probably be more comfortable if this is stitched also. The garment was fastened with a pin or brooch at the shoulder by bringing a portion of the back, folded into a point, over the front. This is done by keeping the back portion taut and allowing the front to dip slightly at the throat. A cord is tied about the waist and the fabric is bloused over it. *(See Photograph 8 and Figure 32.)*

Women and old men wore their tunics ankle length, sometimes with long sleeves formed by cutting the width of the fabric from wrist to wrist with the arms outstretched. It is sewn and pinned on the shoulders in the same manner as described above. It is also pinned at several points along the top edge. Sewing gilt buttons at these points will facilitate dressing and will avoid last minute adjustments.

Figure 32

All chitons are trimmed with an embroidered or woven border from two to six inches wide at the top of the tunic across the shoulder line and at the hem line. It may not be possible to find inexpensive wide trims for the borders, but they may be cut from a brightly colored striped fabric. Or a border may be made using liquid embroidery found in craft shops, or with felt-tip pens.

The chiton was made of linen, the finer weaves worn by the women. They used light pastel colors, shades of pink, blue, yellow, green or lavender. Men wore such colors as olive green, maroon, rust, saffron, scarlet, deep blue, brown and gray. Purple was reserved for kings.

A variation of the girdling which women often wore is illustrated in Figure 33 A and B. A cord or ribbon about five yards long is needed. The center of the cord is allowed to drop down the back to the waist, forming a "V". The two ends are then brought up over the shoulders, crossed in the front, taken to the back and looped through the "V", and then brought to the front again and tied. *(Also see Photograph 8.)*

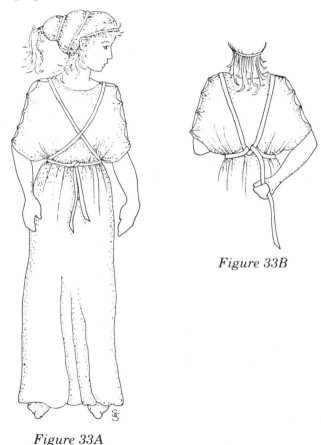

Figure 33B

Figure 33A

The garments for peasants or slaves, male or female, were of coarse wool and drab color, as were their mantles. Men might fasten their chiton over one shoulder only and might wrap hides about their legs for warmth in the winter.

For outer wear, a mantle, known as the *himation,* was worn over the tunic. Sometimes it was worn even without the tunic. It was a large rectangular piece, approximately two yards by 15 yards in size, of wool or heavy linen. The four edges were bordered. It was draped in the same manner as the Roman toga.

Young men, charioteers and horseback riders wore a smaller version of the himation, called the *chlamys.* This was a large rec-

Photograph 8

tangle approximately one by two yards in size, with a border on the four edges. It was fastened on one shoulder, usually the right, and draped over the left shoulder leaving the right arm free. Weights were fastened to the four corners to prevent them from flapping around. Young Timothy may have worn this outfit, as seen in Photograph 8.

Men wore their hair fairly long, softly curled and combed toward the forehead. A fillet was tied around the brow with ends hanging down the back. For festive occasions, a garland was worn.

Young girls allowed their hair to fall softly to their shoulders. Older women often had intricately designed hair-do's. A favorite one, however, had soft curls about the face, with the rest of the hair drawn back into a high ponytail or chignon. Ribbons or embroidered bands were bound around the head and tied at the ponytail. Women might also wear a diadem.

Soldiers and hunters wore the *petasos*, a flat, broad-brimmed hat which was tied under the chin or allowed to hang down the back. This may be made by using a crown of an old hat, cut so that the crown is low, adding a broad brim of cardboard, and painting the entire hat a dark blue. The actor may also carry the hat.

Peasants wore their hair cropped short and wore beards.

Greeks usually went barefoot indoors, but wore sandals of various styles when outside.

Men of this period usually wore only rings. Women wore large loop or drop earrings, pendants, bracelets (coiled snakes were a favorite), necklaces and pearls.

GREEK		
	Male	*Female*
Characters	Young Timothy	Lydia
Style	Basic tunic, short or long. Mantle for out-of-doors wear.	Long tunic. Mantle for out-of-doors wear. Short tunics for girls.
Fabrics	Linen of various weights. Coarse, drab wool for peasants and slaves.	Same
Colors	Olive green, maroon, rust, saffron, scarlet, deep blue, brown, gray. Purple for kings.	Pink, blue, yellow, green, lavender
Hair	Fairly long, softly curled.	Upper-class women; intricately designed hair-do's
Head gear	Fillet or garland	Ribbons, embroidered bands, diadems
Footwear	Sandals. Wrapped legs in winter.	Sandals
Accessories	Embroidered or woven borders on tunic. Pins or brooches to fasten garment. Rings.	Earrings, pendants, bracelets, necklaces for upper classes.

Roman

Nearly every character in New Testament drama who is not Hebrew or Greek will dress in Roman or Greco-Roman style, or will wear Hebrew clothing with Roman touches. The Romans borrowed many of their customs, including their garments from the Greek and for the most part, each garment is an adaptation from the Greek.

The *toga* was the distinguishing mark of a male Roman citizen, all others being forbidden to wear it. It took the place of the Greek himation as a mantle. In earlier times, it was the only garment aside from the loincloth, which a man would wear.

In New Testament times, however, the *tunica* was worn underneath. This garment was cut as wide as the distance from the shoulder to shoulder and two to three inches longer than the length from the shoulder to the knee. The extra length was bloused over the girdle. Older men of rank wore an ankle-length tunica. Peasants and slaves wore only the short tunica of coarse material and dull color.

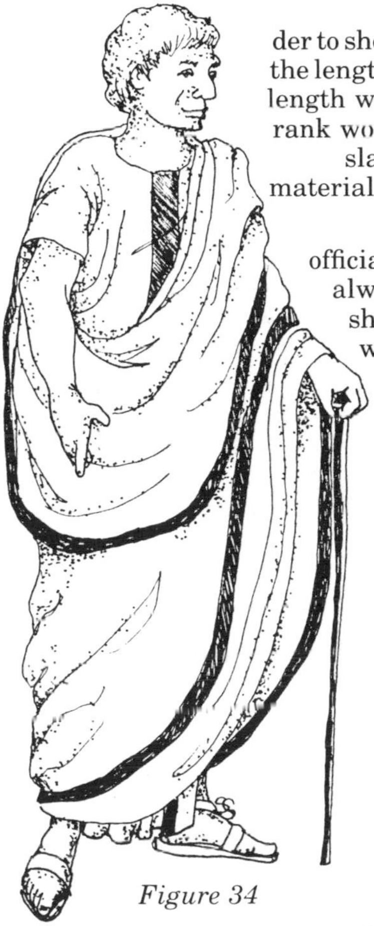

Over the tunica, a man wore the toga for official, ceremonial, or outdoor occasions. It was always white wool, but for stage wear, flannel sheets make a satisfactory substitute for the wool. Magistrates, priests and boys of the upper class to the age of 16 years, wore the white toga with a six inch purple border on the curved edge. The tunica worn underneath had a broad stripe, about two inches wide down the center front and back of the tunica. This is the toga which **Pontius Pilate** would wear. The toga of emperors' and generals' ceremonial uniform was a purple embroidered toga worn over a white tunica with gold embroidery, a very ostentatious costume. *(See Figure 34.)*

The diagram of the toga and directions for draping it may be found on page 46.

Roman men wore their hair much like the Greeks except that it was shorter. Slaves wore their hair long and were unshaven.

Figure 34

Roman men of the upper classes wore rings, sometimes rings on every finger, and usually a seal-ring.

The apostle **Paul** was a man who learned how to be all things to all people. As a consequence, he probably was able to adapt his clothing to the peoples with whom he was mingling. He might wear Hebrew clothing, a tunic and overdrape or aba, when meeting with or preaching to the Jews. And most certainly, as a Roman citizen, he wore the toga when using his citizenship as part of his defense before Roman officials.

Roman women wore the *stola* which was an ankle-length straight tunic, sometimes bloused over a belt. It was made of linen or light-weight wool and in the same fashion as the Greek tunic, with the sleeves formed by fastening the back and front shoulder seams together. It usually had an embroidered band at the neck and hem, and was worn with an embroidered or jeweled girdle. For out-of-doors wear, a woman would wear the *palla* which was similar to the himation and draped in the same manner. Or she might wear a

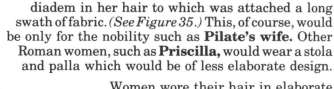

diadem in her hair to which was attached a long swath of fabric. *(See Figure 35.)* This, of course, would be only for the nobility such as **Pilate's wife.** Other Roman women, such as **Priscilla,** would wear a stola and palla which would be of less elaborate design.

Women wore their hair in elaborate arrangements. One style has the hair around the face curled tightly in a "halo", with the rest of the hair drawn into a high chignon. Another style was to have the hair braided and wound around on the top.

The jewelry for upper-class women included large earrings and bracelets. The "snake" bracelet was especially popular. Fibula, or clasps, were usually worn to fasten their mantles.

White was the predominate color for the Roman tunica and the only color for the toga. Other mantles might be of dark blue, green or rust. Women wore red, yellow, sea-green, blue and rust. Purple was reserved for nobility, as usual.

Figure 35

ROMAN		
	Male	**Female**
Characters	Paul, Pilate, Aquila	Pilate's wife, Priscilla
Style	Short tunic, long for older men. Toga for Roman citizens. Short tunic for peasants and slaves.	Long tunic. Palla for out-of-doors wear.
Fabric	Wool for toga, linen for tunic. Coarse fabrics for peasants and slaves.	Linen, light-weight wool, silk for the wealthy. Coarse fabrics for peasants and slaves.
Hair	Short, softly curled. Clean shaven. Long hair and beards for slaves and peasants.	Elaborate, curly. Or braids. Plain for peasants and slaves.
Head gear	Wreaths for ceremonial occasions.	Veils draped loosely over hair or fastened to a coronet for the upper class.
Footwear	Sandals. Slaves and peasants were barefoot.	Soft sandals, often in pastel shades. Slaves were barefoot.
Accessories	A seal ring and many other rings for the upper class.	Embroidered bands and girdles. Large earrings and bracelets.

Other New Testament Hebrew Characters

There are other characters from the New Testament not directly involved in the Christmas or Easter stories as covered previously. Among these are **Paul, Barnabas, Timothy, Nicodemus,** the **rich ruler, John the Baptist,** etc. **Mary, Martha** and **Mary Magdalene** are among the women to be considered.

In general, the basic tunic, long or short, is appropriate for most of the apostles and other male characters. It is easy to vary the appearance through different colors, fabrics, headdresses and mantles. The T-tunic is the basic costume for all, being tied at the throat or left open. A wide girdle or rope of twisted fabric can be worn, sometimes not. A sleeveless aba, striped or plain, can add a different dimension. The mantle or overdrape can be folded lengthwise and worn over one shoulder with the girdle holding it in place. It could also be draped over the head, perhaps covering a small knitted cap.

The kaffiyeh allows another dimension for variety. It can be striped or plain, held by the familiar two bands or a wider swath of fabric, twisted and wrapped about the head several times. Colors should be earth tones, rust or dark shades of blue or green.

Matthew, who had been a tax collector, could be better clothed than the rest of the apostles, at least during the first part of the New Testament stories. He might have some trim around the neckline of his tunic or upon the sleeves or hem of his aba. His colors could be a little brighter.

Judas Iscariot might wear charcoal or dark brown, symbolic of evil and doom.

Such characters as the **rich ruler** and **Joseph of Arimathea** offer opportunities for more elaborate costumes, though still not luxurious. Their colors should be a little brighter, indigo, maroon and dark green. Embroidered borders, braids and trims may also be used. The rich ruler might wear a tasseled fez, while Joseph probably should wear a dark cap on his head covered first of all with his prayer shawl and then a dark shawl.

There are a number of instances in the Scriptures where a clear, concise description of clothing is given, and **John the Baptist** is one example. Mark 1:6 tells us that he wore clothing made of camel's hair with a leather belt around his waist. This was the *sackcloth* worn by mourners through Scripture and was a coarse, rough fabric, black or dark brown in color. Dyed burlap is an excellent substitute and we can imagine that the style was a short tunic, perhaps over one shoulder only, and was very ragged and tattered. The leather belt would not be of the smooth variety, but a narrow, rough thong, perhaps wound around the waist several times and then over the shoulder.

Priests and other pious characters can wear the *phylactery* as described in the section on accessories.

The Apostle **Paul,** as a Roman, could be dressed as such, especially when on trial or in Rome. Otherwise Hebrew clothing as just described is proper.

Young **Timothy** was of Greek heritage and he would undoubtedly have worn that style of clothing, at least until he became deeply involved in his work with Paul.

None of the costumes, with the possible exception of the expensive ones, should appear crisp and freshly pressed. Well-worn is the key word for most of them. *(See the section on Special Effects.)*

Hebrew women's costumes again call for the basic, long tunic. Except for the very poorest characters, the costumes could be adorned with braids and embroidery. Trims were often arranged in a square, surrounding the neckline opening. Embroidered borders can also be used at the hemline, sleeve edges and on the belt. Chains or metal belts can be used or attached to a girdle.

Another style which can be used for variety is the full length

T-gown, belted, with long, full sleeves, such as was shown for Joseph's robe. *(See Figure 2.)* Wide, colorful stripes, especially for the well-to-do woman, would be appropriate. She would then wear a plain, harmonious head drape.

Another gown might be the basic tunic or T-gown with wide, colorful bands sewed down the front and along the sleeve edges.

Colors for women's clothing would include dark greens and blues, rust and orange with occasional touches of yellow and red. Poorer women would wear darker, earth tones. Black would be appropriate for the women who went to the tomb.

Hebrew women, with the exception of harlots, always wore a veil over their heads when they went about in public. These, too, can bring a little variety into the costuming. They should be at least one by two yards in size and may be draped in several ways. One method has been described for the costume of the Virgin Mary. Another is to place the center edge of the long side of the veil at the top of the brow, draw the right end under the chin and tuck it under the other end of the veil which will fall over the left shoulder as

Figure 36

shown in Figure 36. Or the drape can come down over the forehead and then be fastened under the chin as in Figure 37. The drape might have light embroidery or fringe on the edge.

A more affluent woman could wear a little cap under the drape. Along the front of the cap, she might have small gold coins, representative of her husband's wealth, attached to the edge. Bangles suitable for this may be found in many craft shops. Paint black markings on them to give the appearance of coins.

Harmonious colors for the drapes may be used. Cream or off-white is a better choice than white which appears very stark under strong lighting.

Figure 37

Harlots such as **Mary Magdalene** and the woman caught in adultery wore much the same clothing as other women except that they wore no covering over their hair. Their colors were also perhaps a little gaudier and they wore more jewelry. It can be expected that after Mary Magdalene's encounter with Christ, she adapted the clothing of the "respectable" woman.

Hebrew women in general enjoyed wearing jewelry — bracelets, chains and earrings.

Fabrics for Hebrew clothing include heavy to light muslins for tunics, flannel, wool and rep for mantles, and light-weight muslin or gauze for veils.

NEW TESTAMENT HEBREW		
	Male	*Female*
Characters	*Apostles, Joseph of Arimathea, the rich ruler, Silas, Barnabas. Timothy, etc.*	*Mary, Martha, Mary Magdalene, etc.*
Style	*Tunic, aba, overdrape. Trims and braids on the better clothing.*	*Basic tunic or T-gown. Embroidery, braid, trims or fringe on tunic and head drape.*
Fabric	*Heavy muslins, flannels. Coarse for the common man. Brocades for wealthier men.*	*Muslins for tunics. Flannels for mantles. Gauze or light-weight muslins for veils.*
Colors	*Earth tones, rust, dark shades of blue or green, ochre. Indigo, maroon, dark green for upper class.*	*Dark green and blue, rust and orange. Earth tones for lower class.*
Hair	*Long, curly or straight. Bearded.*	*Parted in center and drawn to back of head. Covered for out-of-doors.*
Head gear	*Kaffiyeh, knit caps with prayer shawls or mantles.*	*Veil or drape over hair. Small cap with coins.*
Footwear	*Sandals or barefoot.*	*Sandals or barefoot*
Accessories	*Trims and braids for upper class.*	*Jewelry, bracelets, chains and earrings.*

Reformation Heroes

It is possible that someday a famous guest speaker will be invited to your church to deliver a sermon (monolog). He should come, of course, in the attire he wore while doing his renowned work.

Following are just a few of the individuals known for their influence on early church history and the clothing they wore. Information was obtained from sketches and paintings.

John Wycliffe (1329-1384) was an Englishman known especially for his attacks on the papacy and for his translation of the Scriptures into English for the common man. Although he died peacefully, his bones were later taken from the grave and burned. The organization which now sends missionaries throughout the world to translate the Bible into the language of remote tribes is named for this man.

He is shown in pictures as wearing a long, black-belted tunic with long sleeves and a black cape. His hair was white and shoulder-length topped with a black pillbox type hat. He also had a white beard.

John Hus (1369-1415) was a leader of church reform in Czechoslovakia and was burned at the stake for heresy. A painting depicting him in prayer just before his martyrdom shows him wearing a long, full black gown with a small white collar. A choir robe with full sleeves is a very satisfactory gown for him. A white shirt worn backward will provide the white collar. His hair was dark and shoulder-length. He wore a short, neatly trimmed beard.

Martin Luther (1483-1546) is perhaps the best known reformer. As an ordained priest, he was famous for burning the papal bull which excommunicated him, and for his ninety-five thesis which he nailed on the door of All Saints' Church in Wittenberg. While a German monk he wore the typical *monk's robe* in brown or black with long sleeves and a hood. *(See Figure 38.)*

A pattern for the hood is shown in Figure 39. To make this hood, cut two pieces as shown Sew them together from A to B and from C through D to E. Line the hood with two more identical pieces. An alternate hood shows it closing in the front (from A to B) with buttons.

When the hood is thrown back, his tonsure is revealed. If your actor is unwilling to have his head shaven, the effect may be created by making a flesh-colored skull cap and using rug yarn to simulate hair. Several rows of yarn using the "turkey stitch" is effective. Toupce plaster will hold it in place and may be purchased quite inexpensively at wig outlets.

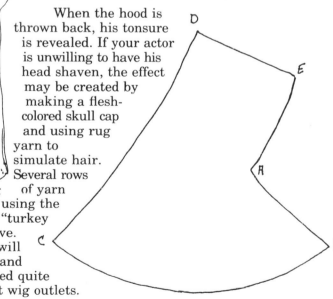

Figure 38

Figure 39

After he left the priesthood, Luther was pictured wearing a short full gown with slits for his arms. Underneath he wore a long-sleeved shirt and knickers which rarely showed. Braid edged the slits of the robe and cuffs of the shirt. *(See Figure 40.)*

William Tyndale (1492-1536), an English leader of the Reformation, was famous for translating the Bible into English. Unable to find a printer in England, he had it printed in Germany and then smuggled into England. He, too, suffered burning at the stake for his efforts. His translation, along with that of Wycliffe, formed the foundation of the King James Version of the Bible. The only portrait found of Tyndale shows him in a black robe. Again, a black choir robe will suffice.

Frenchman **John Calvin** (1509-1564) was one of the foremost leaders of the Reformation in the 1500s. He is most often pictured wearing a long, full black robe which opened down the front. The robe had a fur collar and fur extending down the front to the hem. Underneath he wore breeches. *(See Figure 41.)* On his head he wore a *coif,* a close-fitting bonnet which covered his ears and sometimes a *flat-cap* over the bonnet. Flat-caps sometimes had ear flaps attached, taking the place of the coif. Directions for this arrangement follows.

Cut two circles of the fabric 13" in diameter. *(See Figure 42A.)* Cut a 6" diameter circle from *one* of them. Sew together, right sides together, on the outside, allowing a ¼" seam allowance. Turn fabric right side out.

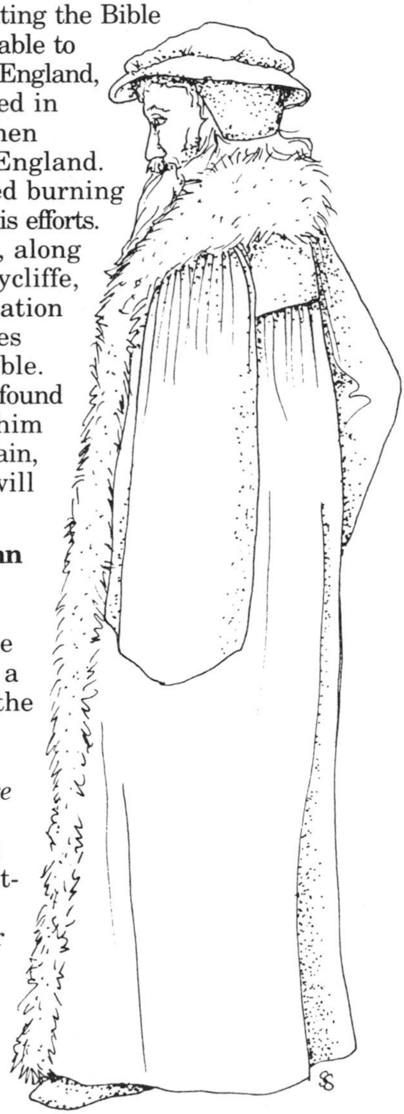

Cut two more circles 10¾" in diameter. Cut a 6" diameter

Figure 40

Figure 41

60

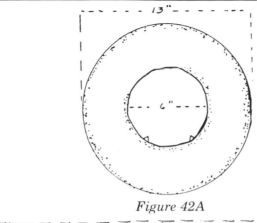

Figure 42A

Figure 42B

circle from *both* of them. Cut an identical piece of very stiff interfacing. Sew all three pieces together along the outside edge. Turn fabric right side out. Attach this circle, the brim, to the larger circle, matching notches.

Cut two pieces for the ear flaps, 14" in length and an identical piece of interfacing. *(See Figure 42B.)* Stitch the three pieces together, right sides together, leaving the notched edge open. Turn right side out. Attach this ear flap to the hat matching notches. Clip seam allowance to the stitching. Finish the seam, either with bias tape or by lining the hat portion.

Adjustments in measurements may have to be made to fit various head sizes. Black velveteen is recommended for this hat.

A variation of the above hat is shown in Figure 41. It is made in the same manner except that the hat portion is cut in one piece and gathered along the outside seam before attaching to the brim.

John Knox (1515-1572), who led the Reformation in Scotland, had been ordained into the priesthood. A painting of him shows him wearing a long, dark full robe with full sleeves gathered at the wrist, edged with a white ruffle. He also wears a coif and a flat cap.

All of the Reformation characters could wear flat shoes as described in the section on footwear.

CHAPTER IV:

ACCESSORIES, STAGE PROPS & MISCELLANEA

Included in this chapter are a number of stage props which may or may not be called for in the script, additional costume accessories, and items which will add enriching details and an added dimension to the performance. Don't neglect these items — they add the frosting to the cake.

Manger

Central in the Christmas story is the manger in which the Christ Child lay. It may be quickly and easily constructed in a collapsible form as illustrated in Figure 43A & B.

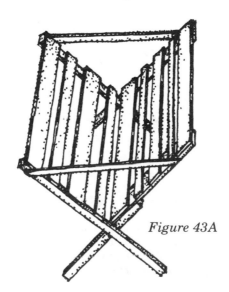

Figure 43A

The "exploded" section shows how the manger is put together. Following is a list of materials needed:

Manger Interior — 4 pieces, 1" x 2" x 30"
                        5 pieces, 1" x 3" x 30"
Manger Legs —   2 pieces, 2" x 2" x 29½"
                        2 pieces, 2" x 2" x 18"
                        2 pieces, 1" x 3" x 18"
Manger Cross Ties — 2 pieces, 1" x 2" x 27"
Hardware —   1 pounds of 1⅜" nails
                        2 (two) 3" pivot nails
                        4 (four) 2" nails to affix cross ties.
                        [Two will fit into slits in the cross
                        ties to lock the manger in position.]
                        1 pint dark stain (or)
                        1 can spray paint

When the performance is over, this manger will collapse and hang flat against a wall.

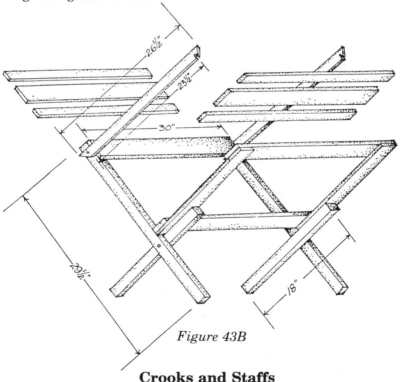

Figure 43B

Crooks and Staffs

An historian has suggested that shepherd's crooks or staffs were actually small trees or branches which were bent and tied while young and supple. They were then allowed to grow and harden for two or three years before cutting in the proper places. If time demands that you spend no more than two or three days creating a crook, you will have to devise something more spontaneous!

Attempts to add a curve to a broomstick usually result in a foolish looking appendage. You might try, however, one of the following suggestions.

If you have a plumber friend who is willing to donate a length of copper pipe, you can bend a curve onto the end. This is apt to crimp at the curve, which may or may not be distracting to you. A second idea would be to bend a length of metal rod and then run it through a section of painted rubber garden hose.

The crook in Photograph 6 was made by attaching a portion of a metal utility hanger from the hardware store to a golf course flag stick and subsequently painted. Flag sticks often break and your local greenskeeper will probably be happy to give one to you.

Shepherd's Sling

The sling which the young shepherd in the photograph is holding actually came pre-made, but a similar one may be made by crocheting brightly colored yarn into a rectangle about 3½ by 2 inches, drawing up the ends slightly and attaching a length of yarn to each end.

Wise Men's Gifts

We have no factual knowledge as to what the gifts of the Wise Men looked like, but the frankincense and myrrh were likely carried in urns, bottles or jars of some sort. In your browsing through rummage sales and your own cupboards, look for interestingly shaped containers. Pottery vases, inexpensive goblets or bath salts containers from the variety store, candy tins, wine bottles (which can have the necks extended with bathroom paper cores) are likely containers for the gifts. Small decorative chests would have been suitable for the gold. If one of the Wise Men's crowns is especially elegant, and of gold, the wearer might remove it from his head and offer it to the Christ Child. These items may be decorated using the techniques discussed in the section on jewelry.

If you are unable to find appropriate containers and must devise them, consider the samples in Photograph 6. The tall urn was constructed by adding papier-mâché over a quart-sized coke bottle, smoothed over with a light covering of plaster of paris, then spray painted brown with a light spattering of gold for highlights.

A slight word of warning concerning this venture — the thick layer of papier-mâché takes a very long time to dry. Don't attempt to make it one day and use it the next.

The chest was constructed with a cigar box used as the base. Half circles were attached to each edge of the lid, then the entire lid covered with corrugated paper. Over this, wood-tone contact paper was used. Finally, gold foil seals from the Christmas decoration counter of the variety store were added for an elegant touch. *(See Figure 44.)*

The small pot was easiest of all. It is simply a marmalade jar, sprayed with copper paint and the lid decorated with a round gold button and sequins.

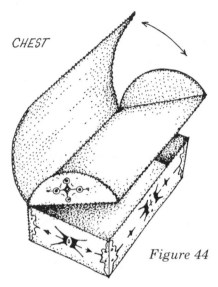

CHEST

Figure 44

Jewelry

Making jewelry for the stage is an enjoyable, creative assignment. Step number one, after the obvious list of what items are to be made, would be to study pictures of ancient jewelry. The library, *National Geographics* and museums are a good place to start. Step number two is to collect ingredients which could possibly be used, no matter how improbable it would seem at first. This would include the obvious costume jewelry which can be taken apart and reassembled in more authentic ways, resins from the craft store, cording, braid, beads, lace (which looks very much like gold filigree when gilded), pieces of felt and fur, artificial flowers (the petals can be taken apart and used individually), buttons, feathers, sequins and even fish bowl gravel.

Tools include scissors, wire cutters, paints, paste shoe polish and glues. A hot melt glue gun is also very helpful to create raised designs and for applying various jewelry components. Foundations for necklaces, brooches, pendants, etc. can be made from industrial felt, tin can or plastic lids or styrofoam. Painted bamboo chains make an excellent light-weight item for jewelry or stage props.

Cut out the desired form from the foundation you choose, arrange the various items in an appropriate design and attach either with glue or by sewing. Gold, silver or bronze paints are suitable for most pieces, but often the addition of black into the background and between bright "jewels" helps the over-all effect. Paste shoe polish can be used to dull surfaces which otherwise are too bright and sparkly.

Brooches may be fastened to garments by attaching safety pins or kilt pins to the back.

Keep in mind that stage jewelry is usually larger and more ornate than modern street wear jewelry. Small items simply cannot be seen.

Nobility often wore much jewelry. Rings were worn on all fingers, including the thumb. Seal rings symbolized power and should be worn on the index finger. Egyptians, Assyrians, Hebrews, Greeks and Romans all wore signet rings.

Footwear

With the wide style variety of sandals available on the market today, and their similarity to the styles of centuries ago, the costumer of biblical productions should find his task somewhat easy in this area. Leather, imitation or real, is appropriate for most modes.

Sandals may also be made from old thongs. To do this, remove the original toe piece and make a small hole on each side of the metatarsal arch (where the big toe joins the foot). A thin key file is a handy tool for this operation. Lace tape, leather thong or rope through these holes, across the instep, under the sole and up through the original thong holes. Then cross the straps at the back of the ankle, bring to the front and tie in back. *(See Figure 45)*. The laces may also be criss-crossed up the leg and tied at the knee.

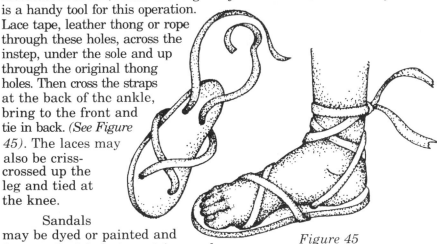

Figure 45

Sandals may be dyed or painted and decorated with designs, trims and "jewels" for upper-class characters.

In addition to the shin guard style for Roman soldiers shown on page 48, the variation shown in Figure 46 can also be used. The sketch is self-explanatory. If desired, the upper lacings need not be attached to the sandal itself.

Roman soldiers and shepherds wearing short tunics may also

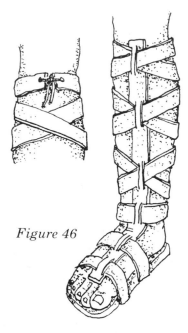

Figure 46

wear leggings with rope wound around the legs.

High boots may be simulated with dyed or painted heavy woolen socks.

The *flat shoe* style should be used for the Reformation characters. It is made as follows:

Cut two rectangular pieces of vinyl or felt. The length should be the number of inches from the back of the heel, under the sole of the foot, up and over the toes to the joint of the big toe. The width should be the number of inches around the foot at the biggest part, over the joint of the big toe. Round off the corners for the toes. Cut a square from the two corners to form the heel. The sides of the square should be the height from the sole of the foot to the back of the ankle. Punch an even number of holes as shown in Figure 47A, allowing no more than one inch between holes. Using a thong of shoelace, lace the heel portion so that it ties at the front of the ankle. Lace the toe portion, draw together to fit the foot, and cut the ends off. An inner sole may be inserted for the actor's comfort. *(See Figure 47B.)*

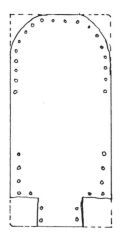

Figure 47A

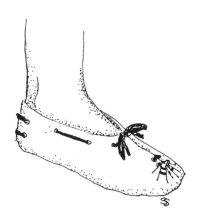

Figure 47B

Padding

There will be times when an actor is much too thin to satisfactorily portray his dramatic part. Padding is necessary but a pillow tied around the stomach is not the best method. A better one is a sack, cut to fit the actor, stuffed with polyester fiber-fill, and tied on with straps over the shoulders and around the waist. Pads will broaden the shoulders and fill in the hollows there. *(See Figure 48.)*

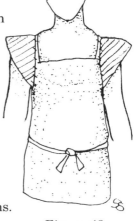

Figure 48

Soldier's Shield

Shields for soldiers from various civilizations may be made by following these simple directions. Light weight masonite is easily cut into the desired size and shape. It may be curved by attaching wire to opposite sides of the shield and tightening with a turn-buckle. Leather straps, one for the arm to slip through and one for the handhold, are attached to the inside. *(See Figure 49.)* The front may be painted with metallic paint or covered with imitation leather. A raised design can be made by applying caulking compound with a caulking gun into any desired pattern and then painted.

Soldier's Sword

Swords also vary from civilization to civilization as to the length, but the basic design may remain the same for stage purposes. The parts,

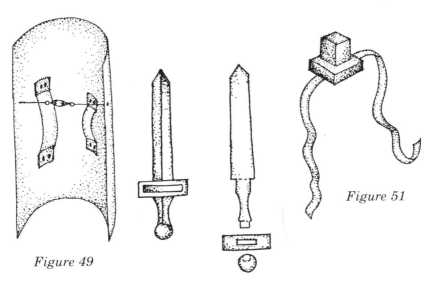

Figure 49

Figure 50

Figure 51

as indicated in Figure 50 are cut from wood, assembled, glued and painted. The Roman short sword was approximately 22 inches in length.

Phylactery

Passages from the law were worn by Jews in a small box which was bound to the forehead by the Lord in Deuteronomy 6:8. The box may be made of black cardboard or painted styrofoam and tied behind the head beneath the prayer shawl. *(See Figure 51.)*

Scroll

In biblical times the Scriptures were written on scrolls as in Figure 52. It may be made of heavy paper, or parchment if available, and wound on dowels with handles and pointed tops, as shown. These might be used in any scene where the Scriptures were read to the people.

Harp

The *kinnor* harp as shown in Figure 53 was the type used by David. It was made of cypress wood and held with the wooden base portion next to the left hip and the left hand holding the larger curved section.

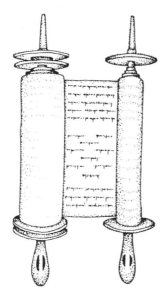

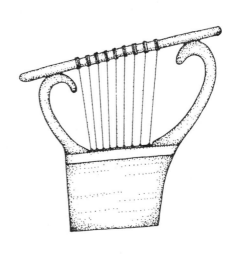

Figure 52   Figure 53

CHAPTER V:

MAKE-UP & BEARDS

Make-up is used primarily for the purpose of accentuating the character's age, health and general disposition. Most biblical plays and pageants, it is assumed, are performed in chancels where no strong stage lighting is available, thereby minimizing the need for heavy make-up. For chancel drama, probably the only purpose for the use of make-up at all is to accentuate certain features for an actor who is naturally very fair and might appear to have no eyebrows or lips at all, or to create the illusion of old age. Light street make-up is usually more than satisfactory for chancel drama.

If one of the characters in the play is to be elderly, or in poor health, use a very light shade of make-up base. Cheeks may be given a "hollow" appearance by blending a darker color just below the cheek bones. Lightly and carefully accentuate wrinkles with eyebrow pencil. But heed this warning — never let an actor appear to be wearing make-up! It is far better to use no make-up at all than to wear it obviously.

A simple way to create gray hair is to brush talcum powder through hair until the desired degree of grayness has been achieved.

If your drama is to be performed with footlights and spotlights, which wash out the natural skin color, theatrical make-up should be used. It is recommended that you obtain a book on this subject, for the techniques involved are much too complicated to be given in detail here.

Beards are created by the use of crepe hair which may be purchased in most costume agencies. It comes in long braided strips and is purchased by the inch. A good selection of colors is available.

The first step in attaching the beard is to unwind the crepe hair and straighten it. The exception for this step would be for As-

71

syrian beards which should be left very curly. Straighten by dampening the hair and then hanging it with a weight attached to the end. Or it may be carefully ironed with a warm, not hot, iron between damp towels.

Determine the area where the beard is to "grow," and apply spirit gum on that area. Cut small tufts of the crepe hair and press onto the tacky gum, beginning with the underside of the chin. This is to give depth to the beard. Then layer additional tufts, beginning with the outer chin and progress upwards toward the hair line. When the beard is the desired thickness, it may be trimmed with scissors to the proper shape. Short strokes with eyebrow pencil at the edge of the beard help to give it a more natural look.

After the performance, the beard may be removed with rubbing alcohol.

The dressing room for the actors will need to have mirrors, tables for accessories and make-up, and racks for hanging the costumes. To the supply of necessary make-up, add cold cream, plenty of tissues, safety pins, combs, bobby pins, and — a large wastebasket!

CHAPTER VI:

STORAGE OF COSTUMES

Careful storage and labeling of costumes will save much searching, frustration and even duplication. Ideally, costumes are best stored on hangers, covered to keep clean. The next best method is to place in shallow, rectangular coat or dress boxes from clothing stores. Fewer garments can be placed in each one than in a large carton, but this makes for more accurate and detailed labeling and less wrinkling.

Costumes should be carefully folded (cleaned, if necessary) and placed in the box. By all means, cover them to keep them clean and dust free. Using a felt tipped pen, in legible print, label the side and top of the box as to type of garment (Wise Man, shepherd, etc.), size and color. Then place the boxes on shelves so that the labels can be clearly seen at a glance. It is helpful to place all costumes of one type together. Then the next time costumes are needed, the proper ones can be chosen quickly.

It is also helpful to keep a record of all costumes. A three by five inch file card, such as the sample below, will enable the costumer of the next production to quickly ascertain if the needed costume is available, must be procured, or must be adjusted.

> **Costume:** *Angel*
>
> **Size:** *32*
>
> **Accessory needed:** *none*
>
> **Note:** *must wear slip*

CHAPTER VII:

GENERAL HINTS TO COSTUMER & DIRECTOR

Long before the final performance, the costumes should be completed enough for the actors to rehearse in them. Many disasters can be avoided by doing so and by considering certain questions:

1. Do the costumes contribute properly to the atmosphere, theme and message of the drama? Do they dominate the scene when they should be reinforcing it?

2. Is each costume compatible with the character wearing it and with the person portraying that character?

3. Are the color combinations suitable and harmonious? Are the colors "right" with the lighting to be used?

4. Do the costumes impair the mobility of the actors? Will they fall apart with the action required?

5. Are the actors able to wear the costumes without undue discomfort?

Full dress rehearsals offer the only opportunity for actors to become accustomed to this type of clothing which is so different from his or her regular street wear. Actors, especially inexperienced ones, must learn to accept the costumes as a part of themselves, to be comfortable in them and to lose any self-consciousness that might inhibit their performance.

And finally, no matter how diligent the director and costumer have been, how ethereal the angels, or dignified the Wise Men, a false note on stage can distract the audience and even induce undesirable snickering. Insist that the players remove such modern conveniences as watches or glasses. Make sure that the men and boys leave T-shirts and trousers in the dressing room. Don't allow them simply to roll up trouser legs — the sight of a pants leg slipping below the hem of a tunic can turn a dramatic moment into a comic episode. Stress to everyone in the production that dressing the part helps the actor to feel as well as look like the character he or she is portraying.

Any dramatic production presented to glorify God's message and staged in his house, deserves the best efforts of all those concerned. The costumer, as well as the director and actors, can contribute beautifully to convey the message and the spirit of the performance. It is an important, and too often underestimated, contribution.

CHAPTER VIII:

COSTUME COMPANIES

There will be times, for one reason or another, that it is expedient to rent or buy commercial costumes or accessories. There are many costume agencies throughout the country, perhaps one in your own community. When contacting them, be certain to allow plenty of time for reserving the desired item. Also inquire about discounts allowed for non-profit organizations. Some companies not only have costumes but carry a supply of other theatrical needs — wigs, fabric and trims, make-up, lights, curtains, scenery, etc.

Following is a list of companies, by state, which have biblical and/or ancient costumes to rent or sell. The asterisk (*) denotes those which have indicated they will custom create a costume to fit a particular need. Other may do this also.

Arizona	Lown's Costumes, Inc. 3933 East Pima Tucson, AZ 85716 (602) 795-5467	*"We do not normally mail out rentals."*
California	The Costume Shop 2010 El Cajon Blvd. San Diego, CA 92104 (619) 574-6201	
	Fullerton Civic Light Opera Co.* 218 W. Commonwealth Ave. Fullerton, CA 92632 (714) 526-3832	

Harlequin's Costumes &
Theatrical Supply*
17 W. Gutierrez St.
Santa Barbara, CA 93101
(805) 963-1209

Hudson Costume Rentals   *"We also have*
11889 Valley View   *costumes of the*
Garden Grove, CA 92645   *Reformation"*
(714) 894-3771

Georgia   Costume Crafters
2879 Peachtree Road NE
Atlanta, GA 30305
(404) 237-8641 (Fax)

Norcostco/Atlanta Costume
2089 Monroe Dr. NE
Atlanta, GA 30324
(404) 874-7511

Illinois   Showtime
2419 B West Jefferson St.
Joliet, IL 60435
(815) 741-9303

Maine   Hooker-Howe Costume Co.
46-52 S. Main St.
Haverhill, ME 01830
(617) 373-3731

Michigan   Tobins Lake Studios   *No costumes. Has*
7030 Old U.S. 23   *large supply of*
Brighton, MI 48116   *armor, shields, etc.*

Minnesota   Norcostco, Inc.
3203 N. Highway #100
Minneapolis, MN 55422
(612) 533-2791

Teener's Theatrical
Dept. Store
729 Hennepin Ave
Minneapolis, MN 55403
(612) 339-2793

Nebraska	Ibsen Costume Gallery 4981 Hamilton St. Omaha, NE 68132 (402) 556-1400	
Nevada	Williams Costume Co., Inc. 1226 S. Third St. Las Vegas, NV 89104 (702) 384-1384	*"We rent costumes locally only."*
New Jersey	Norcostco, Inc. 333 A Rte. #46 West Fairfield, NJ 07006 (973) 575-3503	
New York	The Costume Collection 601 W. 26th St., 17th Floor New York, NY 10001 (212) 989-5855	
	The Costumer, Inc. 1020-1030 Barrett St. Schenectady, NY 12305 (518) 374-7442	*"We also provide a service where our staff will work with student designers on a show."*
North Carolina	The Costume Shoppe 224 Broadway Asheville, NC 28801 (704) 252-8404	
	Raleigh Creative Costumes 616 St. Mary's St. Raleigh, NC 27605 (919) 834-4041	
Oregon	Stage West 12760 SW 1st St. Beaverton, OR 97005 (503) 643-0553	
Pennsylvania	Loeb Costume Collections P.O. Box 2162 Millersville University Millersville, PA 17551 (717) 872-3767	*Rental Only*

Watkins Costumes
718 Hepburn St.
Williamsport, PA 17701
(717) 322-3224

Utah
Salt Lake Costume
1701 South 11th East
Salt Lake City, UT 84105
(801) 467-9494

Washington
Brocklind's, Inc.
500 E. Pike
Seattle, WA 98122
(206) 325-8700

Graight Costume Co.
1120 SW 16th #7
Renton, WA 98055
(425) 277-0440

**West
Virginia**
Magic Makers Costumes, Inc.
940 4th Ave., Suite 360
Huntington, WV 25701
(304) 525-5333

GLOSSARY

Aba	*(ab' a) large, full mantle worn by Hebrews and other desert dwellers*
Candys	*(kand' is) long, full loose robe worn by the Medes and Persians*
Chiton	*(ki' ton) Greek tunic*
Chlamys	*(kla' mis) Greek cape-like outer garment*
Cuirass	*(kwe ras') Roman military armor covering the body*
Fillet	*(fil' et) narrow band or ribbon worn about the head for binding the hair*
Himation	*(hi mat' i on) outer robe or mantle worn by Greek men and women*
Kaffiyeh	*(ka' fi yah) headdress worn by Hebrews and other desert dwellers*
Khat	*(kat) striped headdress worn by the Pharaohs*
Kolobion	*(ko lo' bi un) Greek tunic-like garment, woven without seam*
Mitre	*(mi' ter) tall ornamental headdress worn by priests and kings*
Palla	*(pal' a) mantle worn by Roman women*
Petasos	*(pet' a sos) Greek hat with a low crown and wide straight brim*
Stola	*(sto' la) tunic worn by Roman women*
Toga	*(to' ga) loose outer garment worn by Roman citizens*
Tunica	*(tu' ni ka) Roman tunic*

INDEX

BIBLIOGRAPHY

The Holy Bible

Barclay, William. *Jesus of Nazareth*. Collins-World. London, Glasgow, Cleveland. 1977. (This book has many photos taken from the film of the same name directed by Franco Zeffirelli. It is an excellent source of ideas for dramas based on the life of Christ.)

Barton, Lucy. *Costuming the Biblical Play*. Walter H. Baker Co. Boston. 1937

Barton, Lucy. *Historic Costume for the Stage*. Walter H. Baker Co. Boston. 1935

Davidson, F., ed. *The New Bible Commentary*. Wm. B. Eerdmans Pub. Co. Grand Rapids, MI. 1967

Eerdmans' Family Encyclopedia of the Bible. Wm. B. Eerdmans Pub. Co. Grand Rapids, MI. 1978

Eerdmans' Handbook to the Bible. Lion Pub. Co. Berkhansted, Herts, England. 1973

Elicker, Virginia Wilk. *Biblical Costumes for Church and School*. A. S. Barnes and Co. New York. 1953

Emery, Joy Spanabel. *Stage Costume Techniques*. Prentice-Hall, Inc. Englewood Cliffs, NJ 1981

Ferm, Vergilius. *Pictorial History of Protestantism*. Philosophical Library, New York. 1957

Ingham, Rosemary and Covey, Liz. *The Costumer's Handbook: How to Make All Kinds of Costumes*. Prentice-Hall, Inc. Englewood Cliffs, NJ 1980

Lammer, Jutta. *Make Your Own Costume Jewelry*. Watson-Guptill Publications. New York. 1964

Lester, Katherine Morris and Kerr, Rose Netzorg. *Historic Costume*. Chas. A. Bennett, Co. Inc. Peoria, Illinois. 1956

Lister, Margot. *Costume: An Illustrated Survey From Ancient Times to the Twentieth Century*. Plays, Inc. Boston. 1968

Payne, Blanche. *History of Costume*. Harper and Row. New York. 1965

Peters, Joan and Sutcliffe, Anna. *Making Costumes for School Plays*. Plays, Inc. Boston. 1971 (Many ideas for making stage jewelry.)

Russell, Douglas A. *Stage Costume Design*. Appleton-Century-Crofts. 1973

Schnurnberger, Lynn Edelman. *Kings, Queens, Knights and Jesters*.

Harper and Row, Publishers. New York, Hagerstown, San Francisco, London. 1978

Tilke, Max. *Costume Patterns and Designs*. Hastings House. New York. 1974

Walkup, Fairfax Proudfit. *Dressing the Part*. Appleton-Century-Crofts. 1950

Wilcox, R. Turner. *The Mode in Costume*. Charles Scribner's Sons. New York. 1948

ORDER FORM

MERIWETHER PUBLISHING LTD.
P.O. BOX 7710
COLORADO SPRINGS, CO 80933
TELEPHONE: (719) 594-4422

Please send me the following books:

_____ **Costuming the Christmas and Easter Play**   **$10.95**
#BK-B180
by Alice M. Staeheli
How to costume any religious play

_____ **Elegantly Frugal Costumes #BK-B125**   **$12.95**
by Shirley Dearing
A do-it-yourself costume maker's guide

_____ **Stagecraft for Christmas and Easter Plays**   **$9.95**
#BK-B170
by James Hull Miller
A simplified method of staging in the church

_____ **Self-Supporting Scenery #BK-B105**   **$14.95**
by James Hull Miller
A scenic workbook for the open stage

_____ **Broadway Costumes on a Budget**   **$14.95**
#BK-B166
by Janet Litherland and Sue McAnally
Big-time ideas for amateur producers

_____ **Stage Lighting in the Boondocks #BK-B141**   **$10.95**
by James Hull Miller
A simplified guide to stage lighting

_____ **Small Stage Sets on Tour #BK-B102**   **$12.95**
by James Hull Miller
A practical guide to portable stage sets

These and other fine Meriwether Publishing books are available at
your local bookstore or direct from the publisher. Use the handy
order form on this page.

NAME: _____

ORGANIZATION NAME: _____

ADDRESS: _____

CITY: _____ STATE: _____

ZIP: _____ PHONE: _____

❑ **Check Enclosed**
❑ **Visa or MasterCard #** _____

Signature: _____   Expiration
Date: _____
      (required for Visa/MasterCard orders)

COLORADO RESIDENTS: Please add 3% sales tax.
SHIPPING: Include $2.75 for the first book and 50¢ for each additional book ordered.

❑ *Please send me a copy of your complete catalog of books and plays.*